Vision and Realism

A hundred years of
The Freethinker

JIM HERRICK

Foreword by
BARBARA WOOTTON

ISBN No: 0 9508243 0 5

Published by: G.W. Foote & Co.
702, Holloway Road,
London N19.

Typeset and printed by: Portia Press Ltd.,
56, London Street,
Whitchurch, Hampshire.

CONTENTS

Foreword

The *Freethinker* has just celebrated its centenary. During this long life it has undergone many changes in style and content, but until quite recently occupancy of the editorial chair was a long-term assignment. The first editor, G.W. Foote, stuck to the job for 35 years, until his death in 1915. He was succeeded by Chapman Cohen who had been a regular contributor to the paper since 1897, and remained as editor from 1915 until shortly before he died at the age of 85 in 1954. Since then there has been a rapid succession of editors, largely owing to the difficulties of a paper which emphatically requires full-time service for a modest remuneration.

In its early days the paper was primarily concerned to attack the Bible and to discredit the doctrines of the Christian church. The language used was highly coloured. Thus the Bible was described by one freethinker as "that revoltingly odious Jew production" which "has been for ages the idol of all sorts of blockheads, the glory of knaves, and the disgust of wise men. It is a history of lust, sodomies, wholesale slaughtering, and horrible depravity". Not surprisingly, Foote found himself in prison for blasphemy as the result of comparable eloquence. More surprisingly, a petition to get his 12 months' sentence reduced, which was organised primarily by persons distinguished in "literature, art, science or politics", included the signatures of a number of clerics of various Christian denominations. Foote was being abominably treated in prison, the only reading matter allowed being the Scriptures. But, nothing daunted, his retort in the *Freethinker* was that "Searching the Scriptures was the best cure for believing in the Scriptures".

As the years went by, Foote's own language became more moderate and the *Freethinker* became more concerned with problems of morality. On fundamentals Foote frankly recognised that "morality is based not on logic but on feeling... Reason shows us how to reach our object, but feeling decides what object we try to reach" — in other words, as I have often put it myself, every moral code, religious or secular, ultimately rests on an act of faith. Foote's own faith was based on "the golden rule" and "reciprocity".

The *Freethinker* has consistently defended free speech in all fields, but, in objecting to the censorship of books on sexual matters of an unusually explicit character for their time, the old style cropped up again in a pronouncement that the Bible ought also to be prosecuted. Nevertheless the *Freethinker*'s approach to sexual morality is criticised in this book as exemplifying "the caution of a middle-aged radical" in the days when "Victorian prudery was under challenge from such figures as Havelock Ellis, Shaw and Ibsen".

In the last 15 years of Foote's editorship, as society became increasingly secularised, the original hammering of religion began to look repetitive. But campaigning still continued, notably about religious education in schools. Secularists were (and are) divided as to whether religious teaching should be kept out of state schools altogether, or whether there should be broad teaching about comparative religion and morality. However, all were (and are) agreed that the Christian religion should not be "forced down children's throats" as unassailable truth.

About the turn of the century, some secularists even persuaded themselves that the time for active propaganda against religion might be coming to an end. In an increasingly science-conscious age, the "forces of progress" would, in their view, inevitably undermine the credibility of Christian doctrine. In a sense they were right. Undisguised agnostics, many of whom have never seen a copy of the *Freethinker* or heard of its partner, the National Secular Society, are now acceptable in practically all social circles. But as the century draws to its close, new problems have arisen, not least in relation to the Protestant churches. "Protestantism has become woollier and woollier until distinguishing between a liberal theologian and a non-Christian has become like telling one sheep from the next"; and that goes even for ministers of religion. The result has been that secularist propaganda now directs much of its attack against the Catholic church, whose priests at least stand more firmly by their church's traditional doctrines, on both theological and social topics, such as abortion or divorce. But although the pages of the *Freethinker* tend to be increasingly concerned with social reform rather than with theological creeds, there are still some battles to be won. The unique position of religious instruction as the one obligatory subject to be taught to all children in state-aided schools (in the absence of parental objection), and the retention of blasphemy as a criminal offence are sufficient evidence that so-called "progressive forces" are not self-activating.

The author of this book must have undertaken an immensely heavy burden of research, some of it, no doubt, more than a little tedious. But the reader need have no fear that any of that tedium will be passed on to him or her. Jim Herrick has produced a lively and highly readable story, centered on the life of one unorthodox journal. But incidentally, in his presentation of the setting of that story, he has written an exceptionally fascinating chapter of British social history, covering the past century's changes in beliefs, attitudes and conventions. I am therefore happy to commend this book to others in the confident expectation that it will bring to them as much enjoyment and enlightenment as it has to me.

Barbara Wootton

April 1982

PREFACE

At the time of the *Freethinker*'s Golden Jubilee in 1931, Chapman Cohen, its editor, wrote of its range and influence. He said: "A friend of mine once called it the mausoleum of buried genius. In a sense it is true, in another sense it is decidedly not true. The paper has never had the circulation it ought to have had, one may truthfully say, the circulation it deserved. In that sense the criticism is justified. But it has exerted influence out of all proportion to the circulation it has enjoyed. On anything that really affected the position of Freethought in this country thousands have looked to it for leading and they have not, I think, been disappointed."

This seems to me a fair assessment of the *Freethinker*, and justifies writing its history at the time of its centenary. Amongst the mausoleum of the hundred bound volumes I found much buried treasure. In setting out to write a pamphlet, I found so much fascinating material that I ended up writing a book. There was not time to turn the pages of every bound volume, but I looked in detail at a representative sample and think I have found sufficient examples to demonstrate the range of the *Freethinker*'s approach to religion and the world at large. I was sometimes surprised not to find more about major political events, but I had to remind myself that editors would be assuming that readers read a daily paper and that, while many journals commented upon politics and world affairs, the *Freethinker* was one of the few journals concentrating upon atheist arguments and a radical secularist outlook.

When I reached the last 25 years, I found particular problems. It is not easy to offer a balanced perspective where controversies remain unresolved, campaigns are continued, and individuals involved are still active in the movement. I have attempted to be fair without disguising deficiencies and differences of opinion.

Jim Herrick

Acknowledgments

I should like to express my thanks to three people who kindly read the manuscript and made very useful comments: Edward Royle, Reader in History at the University of York; William McIlroy, current Editor of the *Freethinker;* and Nicolas Walter, of the Rationalist Press Association. I should also like to thank Terry Mullins, Secretary of the National Secular Society, for his co-operation in use of the N.S.S. library, and Barbara Smoker, President of the N.S.S., for proof reading. Thanks also to Christopher Findlay for cover design and invaluable encouragement and discussion while the work was in progress.

Norrie Paton kindly sent me copies of two of G.W. Foote's letters. (The only samples I saw, since his papers have not survived.)

Barry Duke kindly provided a photograph of the *Freethinker* centenary celebrations.

For the quotation from a letter of Bernard Shaw, we acknowledge The Society of Authors on behalf of the Bernard Shaw Estate.

All who study freethought history must be grateful for Edward Royle's pioneering research. I am especially indebted to *Radicals, Secularists and Republicans, Popular Freethought in Britain, 1866-1915.*

I must acknowledge the numerous *Freethinker* contributors, quoted extensively, without whom there would have been no history to write.

Above all, I am especially appreciative of Barbara Wootton's kind agreement to write the foreword to this book.

References:

V. I. — Victorian Infidels by Edward Royle.
R.S.R. — Radicals, Secularists and Republicans by Edward Royle.
See bibliography for other sources and reference works.
All dated quotations are from the *Freethinker*, unless stated otherwise.

CHAPTER I
THE EARLY YEARS

The founder of the *Freethinker* was George William Foote. He wrote an essay "Christianity and Common Sense" which began:

> There are two things in the world that can never get on together — religion and common sense. Religion deals with the next life, common sense with this; religion points to the sky, common sense to the earth; religion is all imagination, common sense all reason; religion deals with what nobody can understand, common sense deals with what everybody can understand; religion gives us no return for our investments but flash notes on the bank of expectation; common sense gives us good interest and full security for our capital. They are as opposite as two things can possibly be, and they are always at strife. Religion is always trying to fill the world with delusions, and common sense is always trying to drive them away. Religion says Live for the next world, and common sense says Live for this. *(Flowers of Freethought.)*

This paragraph displays the qualities of vigour and forthrightness which enabled Foote to sustain his brain-child as editor for 35 years. The sharp contrast between religion and common sense has been the central theme of the *Freethinker* for its hundred years of continuous publication. The debate has not been between academics, but a plain man's debate with common sense as the prevailing temper.

The *Freethinker* has always been associated with secularism (and since the 1890s with the National Secular Society), while retaining a sturdy independence and right to ignore any party line. That melange of atheism and social reform which constituted nineteenth-century secularism — and to which twentieth-century humanism and freethought are heir — contained commitment to a wide range of social improvements. A few years before the National Secular Society's centenary in 1966, David Tribe wrote "A Secularist Charter" in the *Freethinker.* It echoes the early secularist programme while showing the extent to which the charter could remain relevant to modern times. Secularism is neither utopian nor revolutionary; its keynote is "Vision and Realism" to use the title of the National Secular Society Annual Report for 1969.

The Charter proclaimed:

> To make full use of the world's resources and to protect humanity's greatest right — the right to live — there must be world peace. Disputes between nations, as between neighbours, can be solved peacefully and rationally. Moral pressures must gradually replace policies of armed deterrence.
>
> World co-operation is not a utopian dream, but an evolutionary necessity. Tolerance — more, friendliness and generosity — is not to be confused with spineless acceptance of worn-out ideas...Educational systems and ethical codes should emphasise respect for other people...
>
> Just as there should be no special privileges given to an individual on the grounds of religion, so there should be none for an organisation. This means the disestablishment and disendowment of all state churches...

There should be a progressive secularisation of life, in schools, marriages, affirming, and broadcasting "where belief and unbelief should be presented impartially."

The charter indicated that a programme of law reform should include a rational attitude to divorce, to illegitimate children, to restrictions on holy days. There should be no suppression of family planning information and facilities and "legislation for unorthodox sexuality between consenting adults."

> With appropriate safeguards abortion and euthanasia, which are private matters, should be permitted, while the brutal practice of capital punishment should be discontinued.
>
> These reforms are advocated in the interests not of irresponsible libertinism but of a saner and more humane social order, where moral education, stripped of the conflicting and widely unacceptable precepts of religion, will play a more prominent part in fostering interdependence without imposition and hope and charity without faith. (27 March, 1964.)

Such a charter gives the flavour of idealistic hope and concern with the specific details of reform that have characterised secularism and the *Freethinker*. Many reforms have been witnessed in the 100 years of the *Freethinker's* existence and the *Freethinker* can claim to have made a substantial contribution to the public discussion which brought about reforms and a changing climate of opinion. Some reforms are as far away as ever and G.W. Foote, had he been wielding his pen today, might have been more surprised by the influence of the papacy on conflict in Poland and of Islamic fundamentalism on the near East than by the change of individual style and personal morality since the Victorians; he might be more astonished at TV religion and "creationism" than abortion law reform or proposals to legalise euthanasia. But surprise would have been no surprise to him, for he was a fearless thinker, constantly alert to current controversies and world events. His stamp can be felt on the *Freethinker* to this day.

The Background

Though the most long-lived of freethought journals, the *Freethinker* was not, of course, by any means first in the field. The nineteenth century radical press had included much that was severely critical of religion. Richard Carlile was the pioneer publisher in the first three decades of the century in reprinting freethinking, deistic and atheistic works, such as Paine's *Age of Reason* and Shelley's *Queen Mab*. He spent many years in gaol for his trouble, but was an indefatigable propagandist who wrote (slightly prematurely) in his journal the *Republican:*

"The work is done — the press is free
The manner how — here look and see."

An attempt to use greater freedom came with one of the first avowed atheist papers, the *Oracle of Reason,* founded in 1841 by William

Chilton and Charles Southwell. Southwell was an Owenite lecturer who clashed with the autocratic apostle of co-operation because of the latter's paternalism and caution in expressing irreligious views. The *Oracle* at first contained attacks on Christianity more forthright and intemperate than anything ever published in the *Freethinker:* "That revoltingly odious Jew production, called BIBLE, has been for ages the idol of all sorts of blockheads, the glory of knaves, and the disgust of wise men. It is a history of lust, sodomies, wholesale slaughtering and horrible depravity; that the vilest part of all other histories, collected into one monstrous book, could not parallel." (The Trial of Charles Southwell, 1842.) Southwell was arrested for blasphemous libel and sentenced to twelve months in gaol. G.J. Holyoake agreed to take over the editorship of the *Oracle.*

In 1842, Holyoake was himself arrested and tried for blasphemy after commenting at a public lecture in Cheltenham, at a time of economic hardship, that "If I could have my way I would place the Deity on half-pay as the Government of this Country did the subaltern officers." (V.I. Royle, p 78.) Holyoake spent six months in gaol, and although he was prone to assume his experience gave him the rights of leadership which his subsequent actions did not justify, his experience was traumatic and confirmed him in an uneasy, lifelong, radical mould. On release from gaol he established a new periodical the *Movement*, which was much more moderate in tone than the *Oracle* and aimed to "maximise morals and minimise religion".

Holyoake was persuaded by the publisher James Watson to start a new freethought journal in the 1840s — the *Reasoner and Herald of Progress* founded in 1846. The *Reasoner* was a heavy mixture of atheism and Owenite moralism. A period of disillusion amongst all radicals followed the failure of the Chartists in 1848, but the *Reasoner* struggled on and by 1853 was advocating that "Secularism is the province of the real, the known, the useful and the affirmative. It is the practical side of scepticism." Holyoake's search for a word to describe atheism laced with a positive concern for the world led him through Naturalism, Rationalism, Cosmism, Netheism, until he eventually coined Secularism — which stuck.

In 1861 the *Reasoner* failed because of Holyoake's ill-health, but by this time there were other important developments in freethought journalism. The young Bradlaugh had joined Joseph Barker in editing a paper called the *National Reformer*, initiated by a group of secularists in Sheffield in 1860. Bradlaugh's journalistic apprenticeship had been with the fiery *London Investigator*, which collapsed for lack of funds in 1859. The *National Reformer* was able to take advantage of the wave of radical reform in the 1860s — a period in which the Reform League was founded, Palmerston's death was celebrated by radical agitation, and a series of separate secularist groups were given national focus by the formation of the National Secular Society in London in 1866.

There were arguments about how far the *National Reformer* should be a paper devoted generally to radical politics — suffrage, republicanism, and so on — and how far it should be devoted to the counter-theological side of freethought and secularism. John Watts took over editing the *National Reformer* from 1863 to 1866, but his policy of making it a secularist journal rather than a political newspaper was less successful and Bradlaugh returned to the helm in 1866.

Bradlaugh remained editor until his death in 1891 and maintained his intention of producing "an *avant courier* on political, social and theological questions, but never that it should deal with one to the entire exclusion of others". It was a serious weekly paper, sixteen pages of close argument and detailed reports at 2d a time. The emphasis changed in parallel with Bradlaugh's career: "The *National Reformer* has, for this last twenty-six years, been a sort of personal diary in which those who cared had companionship in our life." After Bradlaugh's death in 1891 the paper survived a little longer under J.M. Robertson's editorship, but in 1893 was changed into a short-lived review.

George William Foote

A contributor to the *National Reformer* during the 1870s was G.W. Foote, one of whose earliest published articles was about the poet William Blake. G.W. Foote had a considerable apprenticeship in freethought journalism in the 1870s before founding the *Freethinker* in 1881. He was born in Plymouth in 1850. His father was a customs officer who died when G.W. Foote was four.

He wrote in his "Reminiscences of Charles Bradlaugh" in the *Freethinker:*

> While in my native town of Plymouth I had read and thought for myself, and had gradually passed through various stages of scepticism, until I was dissatisfied even with the advanced Unitarianism of a preacher like the Rev. J.K. Applebee... But I could not find any literature in advance of his position, and there was no one of whom I could inquire. Secularism and Atheism I had never heard of in any definite way, although I remember, when a little boy, having an Atheist pointed out to me in the street. Naturally I regarded him as a terrible monster. I did not know what Atheism was except in a very vague way; but I inferred from the tones, expressions, and gestures of those who pointed him out to me, that an Atheist was a devil in human form. (15 February, 1891.)

Little else is known about Foote's youth. Details of his whole life are hard to come by, and, apart from his career as a freethought journalist, he lived a reticent and uneventful life. He wrote in a letter in 1906 to a correspondent who had asked for biographical details:

> I have always refused to supply biographical details for publication. I regard the modern craze for such things as insane. A man's public life is the world's. His private life is his own.

> I was born Jany. 11, 1850. I joined the Freethought party when I was 19, and worked at the Hall of Science in various ways in association with Bradlaugh. Started the *Secularist* with Holyoake in 1876; The *Liberal* (a monthly) in 1879; *Progress,* a monthly, in 1883; and the *Freethinker* in 1881. Was vice-president of N.S.S. for years. Became president in 1890, being nominated for the post by Bradlaugh. Was imprisoned under the Blasphemy Laws for 12 months. 1883-1884. Went to America, and lectured, and met Ingersoll, in 1896. Have lectured all over the country and held many public debates. Am still alive. — will that do for you? (4 September, 1906.)

This will not do for a man who edited the *Freethinker* from 1881 to 1915, apart from a year in gaol, and who was a writer of remarkable stamina and determination, and a stylist of unusual force and wit. He moved to London in 1868 and worked in a West End Library. His choice of occupation indicated his interest in literature. Poetry was a great love of his and he much admired Shakespeare, Byron, and Shelley. He thought highly of George Meredith with whom he was acquainted. His interest in the arts was wide, including Titian and Turner, Beethoven and Wagner. He also knew the work of theologians such as Augustine and Thomas à Kempis and enjoyed the prose style of Hooker. There may have been a permanent conflict between his literary aspirations and his polemical achievement. He never wrote the *magnum opus* on Shakespeare which he projected. The more general literary and political journals which he edited, such as *Progress,* were less enduring than the *Freethinker.* The respectable literary career which his talents might have brought him was sacrificed to the *Freethinker.*

As a youth in London he lodged with a school-fellow's family, who were "tainted with atheism". He heard secularists, such as Bradlaugh and Harriet Law, on the public platform, and was soon involved as a speaker, writer and organiser. He founded the Young Man's Secular Association and was superintendent of the Hall of Science Sunday School. He was also involved in Republican activities, becoming secretary of the National Republican League in 1873. After lecturing in the Hall of Science in that year he became a regular Secularist platform speaker. (He remained an energetic public speaker throughout his life.)

Foote was an ardent admirer of Bradlaugh, and recalled, perhaps with the glowing hindsight of someone reminiscing at the time of the death of a great man, his first introduction: "It was the proudest moment of my young life. I still remember his scrutinising look. It was keen but kindly, and the final expression seemed to say 'We may see more of each other'." (7 February, 1899.) By 1875 he was, however, finding Bradlaugh inflexible and autocratic and criticised him in the *Secular Chronicle* (edited by G.H. Reddalls until his death in 1876, when it was sold to Mrs. Harriet Law).

Foote joined with G.J. Holyoake in his first editorial venture when the two of them started the *Secularist* in 1876. They parted after two months, differing over the extent to which religion should be attacked, and relations between Foote and Holyoake were cool for the rest of his life. For a while Foote continued with the *Secularist* on his own. An article on "Destructive and Constructive Freethought" clarifies his own view at that time: "No writer in this paper has ever declared that Secularism has not a destructive as well as a constructive work to perform". (5 February, 1876.) However, he was sufficiently moderate to criticise Bradlaugh for "utterances... painfully feverish in their extravagance."

Within the National Secular Society, Foote attempted to broaden the structure of the Society and attacked the office of President, as well as its incumbent, Bradlaugh. The contention probably arose from the conflict between the energy of a rising young man and the dominance of an established leader. Foote was expelled by the N.S.S. Executive and wrote in indignation of how Bradlaugh's imperiousness would show itself if he became "President of the Coming Republic": "A people under his sway would be truly united, for no dissentient would be allowed to live." (*Secularist*, 29 July, 1876.) Further divisions among secularists arose from the disagreement of Charles Watts with Bradlaugh and Annie Besant about the republication of Knowlton's birth control book *The Fruits of Philosophy*. After the trial of Bradlaugh and Besant, there were more criticisms of Bradlaugh (another undercurrent was that not everyone was happy with the prominence given by Bradlaugh to Annie Besant) and a rival organisation called the British Secular Union was formed. The *Secular Review*, started by G.J. Holyoake when he split with G.W. Foote, was taken over by Watts in 1877 and was incorporated with Foote's *Secularist;* it became the official voice of the B.S.U. But the outstanding defence of free speech and the great oratorical gifts of Bradlaugh and Besant, and Bradlaugh's parliamentary campaign kept the N.S.S. the major party and the B.S.U. eventually fizzled out. The *Secular Review* eventually settled in the hands of "Saladin" (W. Stewart Ross) and remained critical of Bradlaugh.

Foote was reconciled with Bradlaugh and the N.S.S. He saw the importance of Bradlaugh's parliamentary campaign and it was at the peak of Bradlaugh's struggle to be allowed to enter Parliament that Foote founded the *Freethinker*. His indignation at the treatment of Bradlaugh by Parliament seems to have fired him into aggressive journalism from his more liberal, literary beginnings. When Bradlaugh was elected as Member for Northampton in 1880, he asked if he could make an affirmation instead of taking the oath; there was some uncertainty as to whether Bradlaugh was entitled to affirm and he prepared to take the oath — but, in view of his renowned atheism, his right to take the oath was challenged, since he did not believe in the Bible upon which it was sworn. So, contrary to many accounts, Bradlaugh attempted to take the oath — on many occasions — and was prevented, rather than refusing to take it. The six-year struggle was dramatic and has been told elsewhere; it made the issues of secularism and atheism prominent in national politics.

The parliamentary struggle made G.W. Foote a militant freethinker. In writing of "Some Characteristics of G.W. Foote" after his death, Chapman Cohen referred to the contrast between the early Foote, who wrote for the *National Reformer* and edited the *Secularist*, and the later editor of the *Freethinker*. The earlier articles were "firm and trenchant" but expressed in "scholarly and studiously polite language": "They were the articles of one who felt the difference between himself and the Christian religion was a purely intellectual one." Cohen continued:

> Talking with him one day, I mentioned this matter of the style of his early articles, and I asked him if he could tell me what caused the change of method. He looked at me for a moment, and then, with a curious side glance said, "I went through the Bradlaugh struggle." That was all; but it meant volumes." (15 February, 1891.)

The Early Freethinker

The *Freethinker* founder trumpeted his militant intention in the first paragraph of the first number, issued in May 1881:

> We will not bore you with a long introductory address, containing a catalogue of promises that may never be kept. The *Freethinker* is an anti-Christian organ, and must therefore be chiefly aggressive. It will wage relentless war against Superstition in general, and against Christian Superstition in particular. It will do its best to employ the resources of Science, Scholarship, Philosophy and Ethics against the claims of the Bible as a Divine Revelation; and it will not scruple to employ for the same purpose any weapons of ridicule or sarcasm that may be borrowed from the armoury of Common Sense. During the summer months special attention will be given to the out-door advocacy of Freethought. Our first number will give a fair idea of the style in which the paper will be conducted.
>
> Any competent Christian will be allowed reasonable space in which to contest our views; and if fuller opportunity is desired, the editor will be always ready to hold a public debate with any clergyman, minister, or accredited representative of the other side.

The style and content of the *Freethinker* in its early days was distinctively sharp and caustic. From May until September it was produced monthly, but was then sufficiently successful to become weekly. The format remained remarkably consistent for many decades. A front page, usually written by the editor, dealt with events and controversies of the day. There were reports, for instance, of meetings to support Bradlaugh in his struggle to enter Parliament. A meeting of the Christian Evidence Society and its scurrilous attacks on secularists was a typical subject for the front page. (June 1881.) A "palaver on Secularism" at the Church Congress in which secularists had been criticised was countered: the Rev. Henry James "complains there is a want of originality about it. Of the Secularist he said, 'The best of the coals that he burns have been dug out of the Christian mine.' We retort that the best coals that the Christian burns were dug out of the mines of Judaism, Platonism, and oriental Mysticism." And another clergyman mentioned the names of Mr. Bradlaugh and Mrs. Besant — "these names were greeted with '*hisses*'. O Loving Christians! O worthy preachers of the gospel of charity!" This is typical of the combative relationship between the *Freethinker* and Christians at the time.

Two regular columns persisted in the *Freethinker* from Foote's beginnings throughout most of Chapman Cohen's editorship in the twentieth century: Acid Drops, and Sugar Plums. Acid Drops were short, sharp comments on the events of the day — usually highlighting what were seen as the illogicalities and inconsistencies of the pronouncements of churchmen. Sugar Plums were the converse, the good news pieces which reported advances of freethought and the worsting of religion. Profane Jokes, also a regular feature at first, were typical of Victorian humour and would no longer be regarded as very funny. Examples from early issues of the *Freethinker* give the flavour of these regular items.

Acid Drops

> THE revised version of the New Testament will be the joint property of the Universities of Oxford and Cambridge. No doubt it will bring them in a handsome sum. If copyright were perpetual, as some insane authors wish, and Jesus Christ had secured the copyright of the Gospels to his own family for ever, what a splendid property it would be! Renan originated this "happy thought." (May 1881.)

(The financial benefits of religion, as opposed to freethought, was a constant theme.)

> THE Rev. John Mactavish, one of the "great gaslights of grace" in Inverness, has made his protest against the profanity of Shakespeare, and been snubbed for his pains by the Justices of Peace. Mr. Walter Bentley had applied for a theatrical licence for the Music Hall, and this so raised the ire of the pious Mactavish, that he ran amuck against theatres, actors and actresses, and even Shakespeare himself, who although a very good writer (for a Southron ye ken) had put an awful amount of profanity into his plays. The pious champion brought a petition from eighty residents in support of his protest. Two members proposed and seconded the rejection of Mr. Bentley's application, and another supported it; but all the rest, to the number of nineteen, voted that the application should be granted. Mr. Davidson, of Cantray, administered a frightful castigation to this charitable disciple of Christ, and the great Mactavish went home again, doubtless feeling that the Lord had once more been overcome by the world, the flesh and the devil. (June 1881.)

(Opposition to censorship of all kinds has been a consistent *Freethinker* approach.)

Sugar Plums

> MADRAS boasts of a neat little Freethought journal called "The Philosophical Enquirer", which is published in English and in Tamil. It is in its fourth volume, and we hope it will reach its fortieth. The appearance of such journals in India and in the Colonies is a remarkable sign of the times. Freethought is spreading rapidly all over the world. (June 1881.)

(A longstanding interest in India is seen in the *Freethinker.*)

THE *New York Observer* says that the May meetings in that city "do not attract the crowds which once thronged the Old Broadway Tabernacle and filled the churches. It is very evident that, for some reason, they have lost their hold upon the people." (June 1881.)

(The decline of Christian worship and the question of whether a revival was round the corner have been constantly watched by the *Freethinker.*)

THE International Freethought Congress, held at the Hall of Science, London, on Sunday, Monday, and Tuesday last, was a thorough success. With one exception the foreign delegates were commendably brief in their speeches. Dr. Buchner, the celebrated German scientist, presided most admirably, and delivered some very eloquent speeches which were greeted with storms of applause. Delegates were present from America, France, Holland, and Belgium. (2 October, 1881.)

Profane Jokes

THERE is a girl in Gloucester so modest that she will not allow "The Christian Observer" to remain in her room overnight. (2 October, 1881.)

"MOTHER what is an angel?" "An angel? Well, an angel is a child that flies." "But, mother, why does papa always call my governess an angel?" "Well," explained the mother, after a moment's pause, "she is going to fly immediately." (20 November, 1881.)

"MY son," said an old lady, "how must Jonah have felt when the whale swallowed him?" "Down in the mouth," was the young hopeful's reply. (27 November, 1881.)

The last, which modern readers would probably find the least amusing, is the most typical.

Other regular aspects of the early *Freethinker* were "Freethought Gleanings" with quotations from writers such as Ingersoll, Lecky, Ruskin, Carlyle and Samuel Butler. There were also historical articles about famous freethinkers, and correspondence which contained controversy between freethinkers and between freethinkers and clerics. There were notices of meetings (in particular, Mr. Foote's engagements) and advertisements for publications like Ingersoll's "Orations", Paine's "Age of Reason" and Hume's "Essay On Miracles" and for Foote's pamphlets with titles such as "Secularism the True Philosophy of Life", "Atheism and Morality" and "The Futility of Prayer".

The extent to which freethought journals should be aggressively anti-Christian was — and has remained — contentious. Foote's determination to use the "weapons of ridicule and sarcasm" as well as "the armoury of Common Sense" must be seen in the context of Christianity in the second half of the nineteenth century. Following the "Higher Criticism" of the Bible, the evolution theory of Darwin, and the philosophical questioning of religious truth, respectable doubt was abroad. But most of the education which ordinary people received presented the Bible as completely true and fundamentalism was a vital force. Mr. Gladstone's reference to "The Impregnable Rock of Holy Scripture", although it does not fully explain his own belief in the inspiration rather than the literal truth of the Bible, accurately sums up a common view. A letter to *The Times* in 1892, signed by a number of prominent Anglicans, called for "A Declaration on the Truth of Holy Scripture" because of the attack on the Bible: "We therefore solemnly profess and declare our unfeigned belief in all the canonical Scriptures of the Old and New Testaments as handed down to us by the undivided Church in the original languages. We believe they are inspired by the Holy Ghost, that they are what they profess to be, that they mean what they say and that they declare incontrovertibly the actual historical truth in all records, both of past events and of the delivery of predictions to be thereafter fulfilled." (See R.S.R. Royle P 171.)

Much of Foote's writing aimed at undermining this view. His *Bible Romances,* which sold for many years, retold the Bible stories in semi-humorous fashion in order to debunk the use of Bible stories by evangelists. *The Bible Handbook* (1888), written jointly with W.P. Ball, contains sections on Bible Contradictions, Bible Absurdities, and Bible Atrocities and has remained in print to the present day. If a lifetime's Bible bashing seems a somewhat repetitive task, it is worth remembering that this stance could only have been re-inforced by imprisonment for blasphemy and a period of solitary confinement during which only Scriptural reading was permitted. "Searching the Scriptures is the best cure for believing in the Scriptures," he wrote in the *Freethinker.* (13 March, 1887.)

On Trial for Blasphemy

In criticising religion by ridicule and sarcasm, Foote was defying a longstanding taboo. He challenged the assumption, which even respectable agnostics held, that religious views should be treated with reverence. He sought to establish that religion is a social phenomenon which should be open to the same range of comment, from vigorous intellectual analysis to polemical jibes, as other aspects of human behaviour.

The Bible Cartoons provided the most notorious aspect of the *Freethinker's* ridicule of Christianity. *The Times* called for the suppression of a French volume of Biblical cartoons by Leo Taxil, *La Bible Amusante,* and G.W. Foote determined to give them wider viewing. The "Comic Bible" Sketches, mostly but not entirely from *La Bible Amusante*, were literal depictions of Biblical texts with a humorous slant. They now seem neither hilarious nor shocking. "Moses Getting a Back View" is a famous one: an old man peers out of a cave at an enormous, baggily trousered back-side engulfed by clouds, with the text "And it shall come to pass that I will put thee in a clift of the rock, and I shall take away my hand, and thou shalt see my back parts." "Jehovah Throwing Stones" shows a group of soldiers running from an old man in the sky hurling stones at them, with the text "The Lord cast down great stones from heaven upon them unto Azeka and they died". Some contained more pointed comment such as "Going to Glory" subtitled "The Murderer goes to Heaven and the Victim to Hell — By Faith ye are Saved", which depicts a murderer with the Holy Bible in his pocket ascending to heaven while a parson wipes the slate of his crimes clean with a cloth marked "Repentance". The victim, unsaved, sinks to hell.

G.W. Foote knew that the *Freethinker's* style and content were provocative. He wrote in March 1882: "No prosecution yet! The *Freethinker* still goes on 'blaspheming', and nobody tries to put it down... Our souls are in arms and eager for the fray, but the enemy won't come on." The fray came soon. Already the *Freethinker* had been denounced in the House of Commons. The Home Secretary, Sir William Harcourt, had been asked by the member for Dover to suppress the "abominable" paper. He declined because "more harm than advantage is produced to public morals by Government prosecution in cases of this kind", but not without agreeing "that nothing can be more pernicious to the minds of all right-thinking people than publications of that description". G.W. Foote wrote an open letter to the Home Secretary, bristling with indignation at the word "pernicious" — "It is precisely the word which Tacitus applied to Christianity". (19 February, 1882.)

The enemy came on in July in the person of Sir Henry Tyler, MP. "We are for it at last," wrote Foote almost gleefully and presumably unaware of the hardship ahead; he writes, confidently, twenty-five years after the last trial for blasphemy, that "we are not in gaol yet, and may never go there. The legal evidence is not very strong, and there are some nice points of law to be raised before the case is finished."

Sir Henry Tyler was a known enemy of freethought who had already tried to put down science classes conducted by Dr. Edward Aveling, Mrs. Besant and the Misses Bradlaugh. The motive and support for Tyler's attack on the *Freethinker* lay in the Parliamentary opposition to Bradlaugh. Anyone convicted of blasphemy was barred from the House of Commons, and it was hoped to catch Bradlaugh, who had connections with the Freethought Publishing Company at 28 Stonecutter Street which had published the first few issues of the *Freethinker.* Bradlaugh escaped the net and in due course proved in a separate trial that he had no involvement with the *Freethinker* issues which were indicted.

Foote reacted to the blasphemy trial with a mixture of excitement, triumph and determination. He brought out his most stirring rhetoric, declaring in a front-page piece headed "Crucify Him":

> Let them do their worst; they will not break our spirit nor extinguish our case. Let the Christian mob clamor as loudly as they can, Crucify him, crucify him! They will not daunt us. We look with prophetic eyes over all the tumult, and see in the distance the radiant form of Liberty, bearing in her left hand the olive branch and in her right the sword, the holy victress, destined by treaty or conquest to bring the whole world under her sway. And across all the din we hear her great rich voice, banishing despair, inspiring hope, and infusing a joyous ardor in every nerve. (6 August, 1882.)

The *Freethinker* of 28 May, 1882, was prosecuted for an article entitled "What shall I do to the damned?" and for a cartoon of the deity entitled "Divine Illumination", showing an old gentleman in the gloom holding a glimmering match to light his pipe. The case was brought against Foote, as editor, W.J. Ramsey, as manager, and E.W. Whittle, as printer. (The case against Whittle was later dropped.)

A second prosecution was then brought against the Christmas Number of 1882, so there were in fact two separate cases against the *Freethinker.* In the second case the accused were Foote, Ramsey and their printer William Kemp. The special Christmas Numbers were a feature of the *Freethinker* and consisted of poems, cartoons and satirical pieces. The Christmas Number for 1882 contained a cartoon entitled A Merry Christmas, Inside and Outside with a cleric's table laden with food inside and a ragged, poor family outside — one of the few *Freethinker* cartoons with any social content. It also included the infamous Moses Getting a Back View, a strip cartoon of the life of Christ and a hilarious "Trial for Blasphemy" by J.M. Wheeler in which Matthew, Mark, Luke and John appear before the court of Common Sense, accused of vilifying Almighty God.

The second prosecution, indicting the Christmas Number of 1882, was brought to trial first and came before Lord Justice North at the Old Bailey in March 1883. Lord North was a Catholic and a bigot. Foote wrote, in a later account of his experience:

> His air was that of a man intent on peremptorily settling a troubling piece of business; his strongest characteristic seemed infallibility, and his chief expression omniscience. I saw at once that we would soon fall foul of each other, as in fact we did in less than ten minutes. (G.W.F. "Prisoner for Blasphemy". *Progress* 1885.)

Foote conducted his own defence and many a sharp exchange took place between him and Lord North. North tried, unsuccessfully, to prevent him from demonstrating that material as blasphemous as that to be found in the *Freethinker* could be freely read in the expensive volumes of more respectable writers like Matthew Arnold and Professor Huxley. In summing up Foote urged the jury to defend free speech, saying that they could be "the last Court of Appeal on all questions affecting the liberty of the press and the right of free speech and Freethought." His three-hour address was interspersed with "frequent bursts of applause, which were promptly suppressed". Despite biased direction from the judge, the jury failed to reach an agreement and a retrial was ordered to start the following week.

Foote and his colleagues were refused bail — a severity which was criticised by the national press. In Newgate Gaol he spent the weekend preparing his next defence. He described his ordeal in Prison Notes:

> My cell is so dark that I have to make a special request for gas, which is allowed. Reading and writing all day on a little flap-table, with my head less than a foot from gas, does not add to my comfort. (11 March, 1883.)

His description of the Sunday in gaol before the retrial is full of irony:

> Sunday morning is a little less varied in one way, and a little more varied in another. In order to keep the blessed Sabbath holy (and miserable), we are not allowed to see any friends, and I observe that the regulation dinner for the day is the poorest in the week. We take our constitutional, however; and as the confinement is beginning to tell on me, I enjoy the exercise more than ever. After the stagnant air in my cell, even the air of this yard, enclosed on every side by high walls, seems a breath of Paradise. I throw back my shoulders, and expand mychest through mouth and nostrils. I lift my face towards the sky. Ah, blessed vision! It is only a pale gleam of sunshine through the canopy of London smoke, but it is light and heat and life to the prisoner, and beyond it is infinitude into which his thoughts may soar. At eleven o'clock I go to chapel. Any change is a relief, and I am anxious to know what the Rev. Mr. Duffeld will say. He is chaplain of Newgate, but I have not seen him yet. Perhaps he is ashamed to meet me. There is no organ in the chapel and no choir, and if it were not for the cook the singing would break down. Mr. Duffeld's voice is not melodious, and although he starts the hymn he does not appear to possess much sense of tune; but the Francatelli of this establishment makes up for the parson's deficiencies. The prayers are rushed through at sixty miles an hour, so are the responses and everything else. Mr. Duffeld reads a short sermon, not bad in its way, but quite inappropriate. Then he marches out, the tall Governor follows with long strides, and then the prisoners file in silence through the door. It is a ghastly mockery, a blasphemous farce. What a commentary on the words 'Our Father'! Now to work again. I feel fresh strength to fight the bigots with. If the worst happens I must bear it, but I hope to win a victory for Freethought to-morrow, freedom for myself and my co-defendants, and humiliation to our enemies.

The retrial, again before Lord North, concluded with a stirring defence of free speech by Foote. He asked the jury:

> to allow us to go away from here free men, and so make it impossible that there ever should again be a prosecution for blasphemy; and have your names inscribed in history as the last jury that decided for ever that great and grand principle of liberty which is broader than all the skies; which is a principle so high that no temple could be lofty enough for its worship, so broad that the earth could not afford a foundation for it, which is as wide and high as the heavens, — that grand principle which should rule over all — the principle of the equal right and liberty of every man. That is the principle I ask you to lay down by your verdict of Not Guilty, and thus close this discreditable chapter of prosecution once and for ever, and associate your names on the page of history with liberty, progress and everything dignified, noble and dear to the consciences and hearts of men.

But his rhetoric was of no avail and the jury was persuaded by the judge's hostile summing-up to bring a verdict of guilty. North sentenced the prisoners as common criminals, giving Foote 12 months, Ramsey 9 months and Kemp 3 months. Foote's response to the sentence has become famous: "My lord, I thank you, it is worthy of your creed.".

The severity of the sentence shocked even those not sympathetic to freethought. The *Weekly Despatch* commented upon those who "profess themselves anxious to prevent the publication of opinions that are offensive to them, and to punish those who publish them..." "...all they are contriving to do is to advertise the former and glorify the latter." Appeals and petitions were sent to the Home Secretary. A Prisoners Aid Fund was launched. Pamphlets were produced: "Shelley on Blasphemy", a reprint of his letter to Lord Ellenborough opposing censorship, and "Mill on Blasphemy". The Association for Repeal of the Blasphemy Laws was formed.

The editorship of the *Freethinker* was taken over by Edward Aveling during the 12 months in which Foote was in gaol. Foote's most obvious deputy was Joseph Mazzini Wheeler, his friend and sub-editor, but Wheeler was prone to nervous breakdowns and was made ill by the strain of the trial. The *Freethinker* columns and Foote's letters show much concern for Wheeler's health while he was cared for in Bethnal House. After recovery he probably did much of the editorial work during Aveling's interim editorship.

Aveling is a controversial figure with a low reputation in freethought circles. He was found to be dishonest in his financial relations and in his relationship with women. For many years he lived with the daughter of Karl Marx, Eleanor Marx, and their unsatisfactory relationship continued until her suicide in 1898.[1] Aveling broke with the freethought movement in 1884 when he was accused by Bradlaugh of failing to repay borrowed funds and other financial irregularities; he resigned as vice-president of the N.S.S. before a motion to remove him from office was debated and became a prominent member of the Socialist movement.

Nevertheless, Aveling was a talented lecturer and writer. He lectured in comparative anatomy and biology at the Medical School of the London Hospital, lectured to freethought audiences on Darwin's ideas, and wrote *The Student's Darwin* and translated Haeckel's *The Pedigree of Man.* He wrote lively front pages for the *Freethinker* and brought wider interests to the paper than anti-Christian attacks: he showed concern for social justice for the poor and for the rights of women, commenting on the refusal of the council of his old college, University College, London, to admit two women to a Botany class.

Aveling and Foote were in frequent communication while he was in Holloway Gaol. Foote's conditions were dire — worse than that of earlier victims of blasphemy law, such as Carlile, who was able to continue writing and editing and was provided with food paid for by his friends. At first he was held in solitary confinement for 23 hours a day and was allowed only the Bible and, after a month, Colenso's *Arithmetic* as reading matter. His reading material was later expanded and after three

[1]) The exact causes of her suicide are not easily unravelled — it seems too simple to blame Aveling's infidelity which was longstanding. The question is examined in *Eleanor Marx, Vol II* by Y. Kapp, where much information about Aveling is to be found.

months he was able to write, in a letter to the *Freethinker*,

> What plagues me most is a miserable lassitude proceeding from the enforced disuse of my faculties. No writing articles here, no public speaking, (in fact I scarcely utter twelve words a day), no delight of battle; nothing but a lifeless monotony, in which the hours crawl by like an endless funeral procession. Yet my brain is still as vital as ever, for it swarms with ideas, and my heart is stout. (June 10, 1883.)

On 24 and 25 April Foote and Ramsey were brought before Lord Justice Coleridge for a third trial on the first charge relating to the *Freethinker* of 28 May 1882. [1]) Lord Justice Coleridge treated Foote and Ramsey with consideration and courtesy and freethinkers seemed to have considered his conduct of the trial was fair-minded. In contrast to Lord North, Coleridge made no objections to quotations from the works of respectable agnostics and Foote pleaded that there was "injustice in the writer in the penny papers carrying off as a scapegoat into the wilderness of Holloway Gaol the sins of all cultured agnostics of the day". The jury failed to reach a decision. A retrial was expected, but the prosecution decided to withdraw the case: reasons for the withdrawal are unclear, but Aveling throught that, with Bradlaugh escaped from the net, Sir Henry Tyler was anxious to avoid continuing legal expenses, while it was also suggested that the prosecution lawyers feared the likelihood of an acquittal under Lord Coleridge and a new jury. Freethinkers saw the withdrawal of the case as a victory. The case established the right for respectable criticism of Christianity by distinguishing between indecency and blasphemy; an important difference was seen between the content and the manner of expression in a blasphemous offence. (The case was quoted in the *Gay News* blasphemy trial in 1977.)

Foote still had the remainder of his sentence to endure. Public meetings were held, but efforts to gain a remission of his sentence failed. A Memorial to the Home Secretary was signed by many people, including Christians. A petition organised by Prince Kropotkin (May 20, 1883) contained a "notable list of names" from those distinguished in "literature, art, science or politics". The sixty names included Herbert Spencer, Leslie Stephen, Francis Galton, T.H. Huxley, Frederic Harrison, George Du Maurier, Henry Sidgwick and Dr. H. Maudsley. It also included clergymen as well-known as the President of the Congregational Union and President of the Baptist Union, and the editors of the *Daily News, Spectator, Manchester Examiner* and

[1]) There is often confusion in the chronology of accounts of the trials. The *first* trial before Lord North in May 1883 was for the second charge against the Christmas Number. There was an immediate *retrial*, after failure to reach on agreement. The *third* trial before Lord Coleridge was for the first charge against the 28 May 1882 issue. The blasphemy charge against Bradlaugh was tried quite separately; it began on 10th April and Bradlaugh successfully proved that he had no connection with publishing the relevant issues of the *Freethinker*.

Liverpool Daily Post. The *Freethinker* contained scathing comment on G.J. Holyoake's refusal to sign the petition.

While in gaol Foote received much encouragement and support from letters, and was visited by Aveling, Joseph Symes and J.M. Wheeler, who reported that despite bad light "Mr. Foote... had gone through such lengthy histories as those of Gibbon, Mosheim, and Carlyle's "Frederick the Great"; in addition to re-reading the great classics of English and French literature. Two living poets of eminence have sent him in presentation copies of their works." (9 December, 1883)

One of the poets was, presumably, Meredith, who first used the phrase "the best of causes" to describe freethought in a letter to G.W. Foote, written a few years later:

> BOX HILL, DORKING, July 6, 1887
>
> DEAR SIR, — I know what is is to find myself standing in the public ways with a printer's block upon me. Your remarks on the verses have given me pleasure. They seem to have violently offended very many.
>
> You carry on a brave battle, for the best of causes, personally profitless as you know it must be, and my good wishes are with you. May they be as acceptable as I have found your friendly criticism! Very truly yours,
>
> GEORGE MEREDITH

Another famous phrase describing the determination of freethinkers came in Foote's last letter from gaol:

> A last word. I am delighted to know that the Freethought party has profited by our imprisonment; it is a consolation. If the Christians only persecute us for a generation, they will complete our triumph and their own ruin. We are engaged in a war in which there can be no treaty or truce. Our policy is clear. *De l'audace; et encore de l'audace, et toujours de l'audace,* — Yours ever,
>
> G.W. FOOTE
>
> (December 30, 1883.)

A crowd assembled outside Holloway Gaol on the morning of 25 February, 1884, when Foote was due to be released.

> For nearly an hour it grew, not in favor with god, but steadily. By ten minutes past eight, when the doors that have been closed upon our friend for a year of life opened, not less than 3,000 people were thronging the roads and alarming the tram horses by their numbers... As he emerged a great shout went up, the first fruits of the cry with which the working class of England will greet this, the most recent victim of our class legislation.

(Not all freethinkers would have used Aveling's socialist interpretation.) Foote was driven to the Hall of Science in Old Street, a well-known lecture hall for secularists and radicals, where a special celebration breakfast took place. Thanking those who had given him such a hearty greeting, Foote said: "They have not had the disadvantage I have laboured under of being out of practice for twelve months."

A few days later Foote lectured to a packed audience on the topic "How I Fell Among Thieves". He was in great demand as a lecturer throughout the country for months. He immediately resumed editing the

Freethinker, determined not to moderate his policy one whit. The Comic Bible sketches reappeared and Foote wrote an open letter to Lord North declaring his intention of continuing to publish blasphemous material:

> Such is my obstinacy! Such is my appreciation of the Gospel of Holloway Gaol! I can only throw myself on your indulgence, and hope you will not relax your noble efforts to convert infidels to the true faith. And in order that you may not lose any opportunity of exercising your generous qualities, I leave this number of the *Freethinker* at your house with my card.

There were no more prosecutions. Cartoons were resumed in the *Freethinker* after Foote's release. In 1889 they were dropped after an inconclusive survey of readers' views about them. Prosecution and imprisonment had given the *Freethinker* and its editor notoriety and great publicity. During 1882 the sales reached 10,000, but despite ups and downs a decade later it had dropped to 4,000 and by the twentieth century had acknowledged that it would never reach a mass audience.

CHAPTER II
FINDING A ROLE

The remainder of the nineteenth century saw the *Freethinker* consolidating a modest position and adjusting its role. It became more closely linked with the N.S.S. after Foote's election as President, in 1890, on the nomination of Bradlaugh who resigned because of ill health and pressure of parliamentary activity. By the end of the century it had outlived the *National Reformer,* and despite intermittent squibs such as W.J. Ramsey's *Jerusalem Star* and the *Truth Seeker* (which became the personal campaign sheet of J.W. Gott), was the only substantial journal of the militant freethought movement to survive. The survival of the *Agnostic Annual* and the growth of the Rationalist Press Association are a different story, but they were to become a major force in popularising the intellectual gains of freethought and scientific humanism.

When Foote was elected as President of the N.S.S. he wrote:

> Do not expect too much from me. The heroic period of Freethought is well-nigh over. Wars are no longer decided by single-handed combat. Everyone cf us must do his share of the work, and we must be content to toil steadily like good husbandmen, who plough the ground, sow the seed, and finally reap the harvest... (23 February, 1890.)

By the 1890s, there were vigorous arguments about whether Secularism was in decline and, if so, why. Comments in the religious press that Secularism was a waning force, and the old standby of atheists converted to Christianity, were countered with ripostes about the vigour and achievements of secularists. Foote could write with enthusiasm: "The dawning of the day of Freethought is over. The sunrise is here," and point to the USA, where the most popular orator, Ingersoll, was a freethinker, to Germany, which "is Freethought to the core", to France, where the President, Crevy, was a freethinker. (7 June, 1884.) In the sense that freethought was becoming acceptable and that secularisation of society was taking place, he was right. Both developments were, however, to necessitate a more modest role for organised Secularism.

Charles Watts commented upon changes which he saw in 1893 returning after nearly 10 years in Canada:

> That Secular principles are gaining ground more rapidly than they have ever done is a fact that impartial observers of the tendency of modern thought cannot fail to recognise. Ample evidence of this has recently appeared in these columns, furnished by the admission of various representatives of the different sections of orthodox churches.

He wrote of the advantages for propaganda in a more receptive period:

> That such a demand exists is an encouraging indication of Secular activity. Fortunately, the public are more disposed than ever they were to 'hear both sides of the question', so it thus becomes necessary that our advocacy should be conducted with discretion, and with due regard to the requirements of the times. (19 February, 1893.)

The necessity for advocacy of freethought to take account of the "requirements of the times" has remained a consistent theme.

The position of freethought was aptly described by J.M. Wheeler surveying "Our Position". He wrote that freethought was necessarily "a minority protesting against the superstition of a majority", but also thought that "time and the stream and tendency of progress are with us." He concluded by delineating a role for freethinkers:

> Freethinkers will keep steadily pegging away till the old superstitions are destroyed. Let everyone who is not out of bondage himself do his best during the coming year to loosen the shackels [sic] of his brethren. (4 January, 1891.)

Foote was often blamed for the decline of secularism in the 1890s, but it was due to circumstances beyond his control — to the uncertain attitude of secularists to the rise of socialism, to the difficulty of older, somewhat prudish people remaining in the vanguard of progress in the age of "new hedonism", to the tangential approach to mainstream politics, to changes in reading habits and education (the age of *Titbits* and *Reveille* was approaching and free education was to deprive secularism of its role as a source of skills and knowledge for working people.)

In the last two decades of the century, from the peak of the "heroic age" around 1880 to the steady "pegging away" of the twentieth century there were many themes to expound: Ireland, the Boer War, and the hypocrisy and idiocy of jingoism and imperialism; neo-malthusianism, the "new woman", and the morality of marriage and sexuality; sabbatarian restrictions, opposition to cremation, and laws of blasphemy and censorship; a host of progressive causes from anti-vivisection to prison reform; continuing republican opposition to the monarchy and the role of the House of Lords; preserving and rediscovering the record of freethinkers in the past and forging new links with freethinkers in all parts of the world; and, above all, the attack on Christianity.

The Attack on Christianity

Foote, as has already been pointed out, thought "Searching the Scriptures" was the best cure for "believing the Scriptures", and a central plank of the assault on Christianity was Bible criticism. This could lead to a mirror-image evangelical anti-Christianity, which depended as deeply upon knowledge of the Bible as its obverse. The relationship between freethought and Christianity could become a form of hostile dependence — though freethought is a wider phenomenon. Once the inconsistencies, illogicalities, absurdities and "obscenities" had been rehearsed in the *Freethinker* a problem of repetition arose. The Higher Criticism of theologians who looked thoroughly at the historical context of the Bible and analysed the diversity of authorship and viewpoints tended to support the freethinker's view of the Bible, but it was to tub-thumping biblical fundamentalism that the *Freethinker* paid the most attention.

Joseph Symes echoed Foote in a piece entitled "Search the Scripture": "It is my long-standing conviction that the more the Bible is read the less it will be believed." In typical *Freethinker* style he then refers to faith in the Bible as "one of the most debasing and mischievous of sentiments". He then makes some comments upon Matthew's Gospel "merely to set the reader thinking for himself". (30 March, 1884.) The following textual criticism may stand for innumerable pages of the early *Freethinker:*

> Chapter II.—*There came wise men* (Magi) *from the east to Jerusalem* (v.,21) What a story!Who were these magi? Persian fire-worshippers were called by that name. Did they visit Jerusalem and speak to Herod, and Josephus not mention it? They were guided by a star — to the wrong place. Divine guides always lead astray. The star conducted them to Jerusalem, were [sic] Jesus was not born; they had to get other guides to reach Bethlehem...
>
> Chapter III.—*In those days came John the Baptist,* etc. (v.1)—In what days? This has the air of history at first sight; reflexion finds it indefinite and misleading. You would suppose he meant the days referred to in the former chapter. Read on, and you discover your error...
>
> Chapter IV. ....
>
> *He fasted forty days,* etc. (v.2)—How do you vouch for that, Matthew? If he did so, he must have been insane to begin with, or else the fast produced a species of *deliriums tremens.* The whole story of the temptation would be to-day treated as a serious case of mania, and the patient placed under medical care and restraint. Had medical skill two thousand years ago been what it is now, Jesus and his paltry revelations would never have been heard of — except as a specimen of what insane musings could produce. Nothing could be more ridiculous than the temptation. If Jesus was all-wise and all-mighty, then temptation was not real; it could make no impression. If he was what orthodoxy says, he *could not* have sinned, and therefore to submit to the show of temptation was merely a farce. A farce when played as such, may have a legitimate function — viz., to instruct and amuse; a farce performed as a serious thing is hypocrisy, an imposition; and such was Christ's temptation, if orthodoxy is correct. (30 March, 1884.)

The impudence and sense of excitement at castigating and tearing apart the Holy Writ are no longer easy to appreciate.

J.M. Wheeler offered a more scholarly analysis in the same issue. In an article about *New Testament Corruptions* he uses Dr. Scrivener's *Plain Introduction to the Criticism of the New Testament* and refers to Origen's comment upon the diversity of early texts. He quotes Celsus, "the early opponent of Christianity", who "boldly says the Christians 'altered the gospel three or four different times, as if they were drunk, and, when pressed by their adversaries, referred to that reading which best suited their purposes'." Wheeler adds, "This latter practice of primitive Christians has not been lost on their devoted followers."

Whether couched in the challenging, mocking tones of Symes or the patient, gentle voice of Wheeler, such criticism of the Bible ultimately became monotonous once the truth and authority of the Bible were no longer accepted. Shaw said "Bible-smashing is tedious to people who have smashed their Bibles." (1 November, 1908.) But the smashing must have been part of the excitement for the first two decades of the *Freethinker's* history.

The secularists took the Protestant belief that the Bible should be read and interpreted by the individual to its ultimate, logical conclusion. "No wonder," wrote Foote, "the Catholic Church looks upon Bible reading by the layman as a dangerous practice. It has always tried to keep the sacred volume in the hands of the priests... But the Protestant Church, by putting the Bible in the people's hands, opened a broad road to heresy, and flung Christianity into the melting-pot." (13 March, 1887) This view was emphasised in an unsigned piece, "An Abominable Roman Catholic Book":

> The truest and most real religion is the Roman Catholic. We know that this is to the average Protestant a very irritating remark. It is none the less true. The English Church and all the dissenting sects are but bastard imitations of the veritable religion. They are poor compromises between religion and Freethought. They are fainthearted steps in the direction of liberty. (1 July, 1883.)

(The abominable book was the *Pearls of Saint Francois de Sales* — the reaction to which demonstrates the ambivalence with which freethinkers hovered between prudery and sarcasm: "These verses are so vile that not only dare we not translate them, we dare not print them even in the French tongue in which they are written. The Song of Solomon is a chaste and prudish production by the side of this volume intended for the use of young girls.")

The history of Christianity, as well as Biblical criticism, was used to debunk the idea that its progress was guided by God. Christmas time regularly brought articles on the pagan origins of Christmas. Persecution of heretics and freethinkers by Christians were often recalled and wars of religion instanced to demonstrate the evils of religion. For example, an article headed "True Christian Love" (9 October, 1881) gave a lurid account of the massacre of St. Bartholomew.

The *Freethinker*'s favourite enemies were those organisations which defended the literal truth of Christianity. The Christian Evidence Society was founded in 1870 to combat "the present prevalence of scepticism or unbelief in various classes of society." A similar organisation, with less respectable backing, was the Anti-Infidel League, which was run by Charles Bradlaugh's younger brother, William, who had taken to drink but then signed the pledge and been converted by Moody and Sankey. The *Freethinker* reserved its most forthright and vitriolic attacks for such extreme fundamentalist organisations, the acrimony being fuelled by the smear tactics which were encountered. Chapman Cohen, who met with much personal abuse in open air meetings from members of organisations like the Christian Evidence Society, called them "unscrupulous and foul-mouthed liars." (Autobiography.) Foote demonstrated the *Freethinker's* strength of feeling about such tactics:

> The fashion is set from above; and the malignity which concocts and circulates lists and stories of 'converted infidels' is the same in kind as that which animates the lower dabblers in libel who bespatter Freethinkers with Christian filth. (6 June, 1886.)

The meetings of Moody and Sankey, the American evangelical duo, were lampooned, and a visiting American preacher, Dr. Talmage, dubbed "A Pious Mountebank" in a front-page account of his sermons:

> He preaches in America, in a place which profane persons call 'the Jabbernacle'. They reckon that you hear more sound and less sense in that building than in any other in the United States. The great Talmage has a world-wide reputation. He visited England a year or two ago and lectured in our great towns. He also cleared out the excequers of half the Young Men's Christian Associations in the country. There is no need for him to sing "Remember me". His sermons are published in religious journals here for the benefit of souls and of their 'great circulation'. Greater trash was hardly ever printed, but Talmage has a wonderful faculty for pouring out floods of sensational rhetoric, and this makes him popular. Metaphorically, he jumps, capers, stands on his head, and turns summersaults. He is one of the cleverest pulpit mountebanks in the world. (9 October, 1891.)

If this criticism seems to lack intellectual rigour, Dr. Talmage had a similar approach: "He (the believer) has 'an infallible Bible, a supernatural religion, a divine Christ, in whom all the world must be saved or lost.' About this, he very justly observes, 'no elaborate thinking is necessary'."

Foote was particularly contemptuous of Booth's Salvation Army, writing a pamphlet replying to Booth called "Salvation Syrup; or Light on Darkest England." An Acid Drop reveals Foote's view of the Sally Army (and the whole of Christianity):

> Lord Shaftesbury writes to the Countess Gasparin that the Salvation Army 'seems to him to be the work of the Devil, who having for a long time tried to render Christianity odious, has changed his tactics and is attempting to make it ridiculous.' We differ from his lordship, No one, not even the Devil, could possibly make Christianity more odious and ridiculous than it is. (4 March, 1883.)

By contrast, Foote admired the subtlety of Newman's thinking. Foote was always ready to admire fine theological prose. Newman was also admired for not supporting the blasphemy trial, and for not arguing with atheists. If the rough and tumble of polemical debate could lead to abusive epithets like "odious and ridiculous", Foote also urged study and sympathy, writing on the death of Cardinal Newman: "And if Atheists who study Newman are struck by his saintliness, if they find that the champion of superstition is terribly strong and adroit, it will be a double lesson to them — first, in human sympathy, and secondly, in the perfecting of their own weapons and methods of warfare." (11 August, 1890.)

Philosophical arguments about religion were printed, though short statements intended to speak for themselves were often substituted for extended analysis. The readership, after all, did not consist of professors of philosophy. An example of a quotation presumed to speak for itself was Schopenhauer's sentence, "Religions are like glow-worms, they shine in the dark."

A frequent argument used to demonstrate that the Church was not infallible and God did not look after his own was found in a stream of stories about clerical suicides, heart attacks while at prayer in church, and steeples struck by lightning. An Acid Drop on 10 February 1895 recounts how "A church at Marsala was unroofed during a cyclone, and a marriage being in progress, the bride was fatally crushed by the falling debris."

Disasters, which suggested to freethinkers the impossibility of believing in an omnipotent, all-loving deity, were a common theme. The death of many children in an accident in a Sunderland hall (the article leaves the cause unclear, presumably because it was headline news at the time) showed to Aveling

> the difficult task of reconciling the wholesale slaughter of innocent children with the omniscience and omnipotence of an all-good god... That god, on the Christian theory, is directly responsible for the holocaust of victims in a Sunderland hall no man can deny save those who are godless... The criminal is god... So strange that infatuated ones are willing to ascribe to him all good and are unwilling to attribute to him all evil! (15 July, 1883.)

Also in reaction to disaster, a cholera epidemic in France and Naples evinced a complaint from the *Freethinker* that people resort to prayer and figures of saints, rather than medicine and hospitals.

In a front page on Miracles in 1886, Foote refers to Hume's essay on Miracles and demonstrates that more detailed philosophical argument was not neglected in the *Freethinker*. Current science and anthropology were referred to, even if they were not the staple diet of *Freethinker* readers. Aveling was an excellent populariser of Darwin's theories, his book *The Student's Darwin* (1881) being advertised for sale for many years. A front-page article on 10 January, 1886, was devoted to the controversy between Gladstone and Huxley about evolution and the origins of the universe. Considerable attention was given to the writings of Huxley, and on the deaths of Darwin and Huxley the *Freethinker* praised these men and emphasised the implications of ideas of evolution. There was a tendency to concentrate upon the controversies and the anti-theological implications of evolution rather than the biological details.

Materialism, or the belief that there is no non-material basis to thought or mind, was a crucial freethought position. The relevance of evolution to the development of intelligence was seized upon: W.P. Ball asked, "Can a non-intelligent cause produce an intelligent effect?", and suggested that "The gradual evolution of intelligence has obviously been brought about by the struggle for existence and the survival of the fittest through innumerable generations." (29 September, 1889.) Monism in which "the traditional dualism of mind and matter was abolished, not in favour of matter, but in favour of one substance incorporating what had traditionally been called mind and what had traditionally been called matter" (R.S.R. Royle, p 172) was important to Chapman Cohen and its exposition in Haeckel's *Riddle of the Universe* (published by the R.P.A. in 1900) became popular among freethinkers in the early twentieth century.

The details of philosophy and science do not loom large in a paper intended as a popular weekly, but attentive readers were given quite enough short pieces to follow up if they wished. Probably more important was a general commitment to scientific development, lucidly expressed in an article by Wheeler on "Science and Religion": "The basis of science is entirely different from that of religion. Religion is stationary; science progressive. The only peace (between science and religion) possible is by the constant surrender of religion to science, and the accommodation of the theories of the former to those of the latter." (28 April, 1895.)

Liberal Christians whose theology adjusted to changes in intellectual currents were seen by the *Freethinker* as traitors to true Christianity too timid to abandon it completely. The description of Unitarianism by Darwin's grandfather, Erasmus Darwin, provided a favourite quote — "a feather-bed to catch a falling Christian".

Criticism of Christianity was allied with an increasing awareness of other religions, often compared favourably with Christianity. In an article comparing Buddha and Christ J.M. Wheeler finds Buddha the more impressive figure, but also makes a more important general point: "Among the causes which have led to unbelief in the supernatural claims of Christianity must be reckoned the knowledge which has of late years been unearthed concerning the rival claims of other beliefs." (31 January, 1886.) The intolerance of one religion towards another also encouraged a challenge to the claims of any one religion to hold the divine truth. In a comment, which has an unhappily modern ring, an incident involving Moslems in Liverpool is cited as an example of Christian intolerance: Moslems were prevented from "performing devotions in peace" by snowballs containing stones being hurled at those entering the mosque.

Minor religions and superstitions were debunked as well as the major religions. Theosophy was given thorough attention because one of its leaders, Mrs. Besant, was a prominent former secularist. There was much comment on revelations concerning forged letters among Theosophists after an exposure in the *Westminster Review* in 1895: Mrs. Besant claimed to have been duped and the *Freethinker* declared: "Dabblers in the 'occult' are sure to get more or less corrupted... they deceive themselves and they deceive others..." (20 January, 1895.)

Far less attention was paid to the presentation of atheism than might be expected. Atheism, once religion has been dealt with, became a presumption. The atheist "cause" was indirectly served by homage to freethought martyrs. The heretic, Giordano Bruno, was admired for the courage with which he faced the flames and Foote wrote a poem about him (no doubt conscious of comparisons) while he was in prison; a front page on 25 February, 1900, four hundred years after Bruno's death, trumpets "The Greatest of Freethought Martyrs".

Underlying the entire critique of religion were deeply held assumptions about the harmful effects of religion. The "sky-pilots", as priests were labelled, were guiding people to an illusion. "We war with Christianity, for its fruits past and present show it to be the upas-tree of evil. Look upon Christianity — see the barnacles of blood, human blood, that encrust and adorn it, and have smeared it for ages..." (17 February, 1884.) The imminent death of Christianity was a subject for joy:

> Freethinkers, be joyous and gay, for the creed
> Of Christ on its deathbed is lying,
> And soon from its presence mankind will be freed.
> Great news — Christianity's dying!
>
> (S.J. Bellchambers. 17 February, 1884.)

The world picture of the freethinker was sustained not by gloating triumph over Christianity, but by a belief in progress: Charles Watts wrote of "The Value of Doubt" concluding that "In proportion as doubt has been fostered, progress has been followed, and mental liberty has been vindicated." (5 May, 1895.)

Both an assumption that religions were likely to wither away and that humanity is on a steady path of progress have been impossible to sustain in the twentieth century.

The Freethinker and Politics

"We do not discuss politics in the *Freethinker*, but Education is not a political question..." wrote Foote in a piece on secular education. (24 October, 1886.) Foote's belief that the *Freethinker* was not political explains the absence of detailed discussion of major political questions of the day. This was partly due to Foote's concern not to split secularists, whose political views were varied, and partly due to his belief that the *Freethinker's* aim was to concentrate upon matters of religion. Commentary upon the new Parliament elected in 1900 read:

> ... the moulding of public opinion is a far more important thing than the election of representatives. They really rule who influence the mind of the electors, including all the women in the kingdom. We would rather occupy the editorial chair of this journal than a seat in the House of Commons. We would rather be a force than a register — a cause than the most conspicuous effect. (7 October, 1900.)

Foote's views might have been different if he had been more actively involved in politics. He nearly became a Liberal candidate for Walworth in 1884, but the selection committee chose another radical by 26 votes to 22, and the *Freethinker* report hints that Foote's atheism told against him. The *Freethinker,* while being "non-political", broadly favoured the

Liberal approach, though it became increasingly critical of Gladstone, especially for his religious views. Foote preferred moulding public opinion by editing to ruling as a representative of the people, but he firmly supported parliamentary democracy. He had some of the self-made, working-class, auto-didact's doubts about the wisdom of the masses, writing in a review of Kropotkin's *Expropriation. An Anarchist Essay* that "its doctrine is a very hazardous one to preach to people who are unemployed and starving".

Foote was not himself convinced by socialism, into which much radical energy was poured in the 1890s, but was reluctant to criticise it in the columns of the *Freethinker.* His view was judiciously put in a note added to a letter taking Foote to task for criticising socialism: "The passage he [the letter writer] quotes is not an attack on Socialism, but simply a warning against accepting without discussion, as flies dash at a treacle-pot... But while not attacking Socialism in this journal, which is devoted to quite other purposes, we have always given our readers to understand that we are not socialist." (11 October, 1885.) He had also written in an article on "Freethought and Socialism" that the *Freethinker* placed emphasis on freeing man's mind from superstition first: "We must free men's minds before we can free their bodies." This belief in the power of propaganda to change minds as a prerequisite of a better society was an enduring and important part of the freethought tradition.

Among the "non-political" issues which the *Freethinker* often returned to was Ireland — seen as essentially a religious problem. The *Freethinker's* support for Home Rule, believing in self-autonomy and freedom, was tempered by a fear that in Ireland Home Rule would mean Rome Rule. A cartoon headed Home Rule showed a Roman Catholic priest riding a pig, labelled Ireland. The caution about the dangers of Roman control were "not a plea against Home Rule for Ireland". (20 June, 1886.) At the same time a somewhat simple-minded optimism suggested — "The Irish are a quick-witted race, and when Freethought once creeps among them it will spread like fire."

The general point that religious hostilities conflict with religious claims of benevolence was often made. An Acid Drop of 25 July 1886 could almost be repeated 100 years later with equal point: "A man during one of the Belfast riots, was asked by a mob what his religion was. He didn't know whether his interrogators were Catholics or Protestants, but he looked at their weapons, their bludgeons, and their revolvers, surveyed all carefully, and answered — 'Gentlemen, I am of the same opinion as that man there with the big axe'."

When Parnell stood in an election in Kilkenny, following the scandal of his divorce, comment began with the usual disclaimer: "This is a Freethought journal, pure and simple, and we have no concern with the political issues of the Kilkenny election." But the front page article continued its attack on Catholicism:

> the greatest curse of Ireland... The people are trained up as political slaves,

> and this is the real secret of their political dependence. So far from being rebels, the Irish are the most easily governed, ay, and the most easily coerced, of European nations. Had the power of the priest been broken, had the Irish been mentally free, they would long ago have asserted and secured their civil liberties.

The divorce scandal was not the main point. "Debauching another man's wife is bad enough, no doubt; but it is not so bad, after all, as systematically debauching the mind of a whole nation from the cradle to the grave." (4 January, 1891.)

In other conflicts the *Freethinker* was prone to comment on the irony of warring Christian groups, rather than analyse the complete situation. The Boer Wars, for instance, led to a caution against the "rush into the frightful crime of an avoidable war" and bitter amusement at the sight of two Christian nations fighting each other. The *Freethinker* was anti-war, without being specifically pacifist, critical of imperialism, and likely to oppose an ideal of the brotherhood of man to what was seen as the warring religious spirit. After the death of General Gordon at Khartoum, Foote referred to "patriotic fever" and "the Jingoes" and sarcastically supposed "we shall go on appropriating the world at our leisure." There was no sympathy for the dead General, whose Christian views were well-known, and disapproval of the exaggerated picture of Islamic barbarity. "The future historian of our age will probably relate that, as usual, the Cross outdid the Crescent in slaughter, and added to its guilt the meanness of hypocrisy." Bradlaugh and Foote spoke at a demonstration meeting against the Sudan War at St. James's Hall.

A front page "War and Humanity" commented on the second Boer War and concluded with an appeal to humanity:

> We must pity the poor wounded on our own side, and we pity still more the widows and fatherless children of the dead. We also pity the poor wounded Boers, and the widows and orphans in many a far-off Transvaal farm. Human feelings are much the same everywhere, and suffering and grief on all sides call for our compassion.
>
> ...It is this (Tommy Atkins) spirit of human fellowship, deep down in men's hearts, that gives the best hope for the future. How much of the quarrelling and fighting in the world is, after all, the result of mere misunderstanding! If we could only get to know each other more, we should be better friends. It is mutual intimacy that must lead to the fraternisation of the peoples. (26 November, 1899.)

From its beginning the *Freethinker* took an interest in India and was critical of imperialism. "We lay the flattering unction to our souls that we seek to govern India for its own benefit. But facts speak louder than pretences." (Acid Drop, 5 March, 1882)

"The God of Battles" was the title of a cartoon and an article, which sums up the early *Freethinker's* attitude to war: the occasion was the threat of war between England and Russia, between Mr. Gladstone and the Tsar:

> Ostensibly they are wrangling about a paltry strip of useless territory in Central Asia, but the real cause of their mighty difference lies in their

> egoism and obstinacy... They manifest in a 'civilised' manner all the petty feelings which animate a couple of scolding shrews, and all the dark passions of a couple of brawling costermongers. Both these eminent gentlemen, however, are ardent Christians, humble disciples of the Prince of Peace. (3 May, 1884.)

The *Freethinker* was no more complimentary about aristocratic princes and royalty. The fierce republicanism of the 1870s had subsided by the time of Queen Victoria's jubilee in 1897, though the *Freethinker* mustered some sharp comment upon the service of thanksgiving in Westminster Abbey: "Had she been sixty-eight at her coronation, there would have been something miraculous in her jubilee..." The vulgarity of the preaching was criticised: "Not a word about the royal family being wise, virtuous and useful. It is simply 'O Lord give them treacle here, and treacle hereafter. Amen'." Victoria's death in 1901 brought the grudging comment, she was "doubtless a good woman... Still, we hope this is no distinction in England. We believe there are hosts of good women in the country..." and there was no time for the newspapers which "have been going it blind... Unlimited gush was the order of the day." (26 June, 1897.)

Criticism of the monarchy which had been a personal attack on the extravagance and dissipation (the *Freethinker* could be somewhat puritanical) of royal and aristocratic individuals contained a more important component of attack on land ownership and the hierarchy of political power. The House of Lords was included in such strictures, and the opposition to the Deceased Wife's Sister's Bill in 1882 provoked the *Freethinker* to use a quote from the *Church Reformer*, which expressed a typical freethought view: "The presence of the bishops in the House of Lords is of very doubtful advantage to the Church, and is positively injurious to the national progress." (The *Church Reformer* of Stewart Headlam, a Christian socialist, was hardly typical.)

The individual political reforms which the *Freethinker* persisted in calling for included the abolition of the blasphemy law, the right to affirm for MPs (achieved by Bradlaugh) the abolition of laws prohibiting Sunday activities, and cremation ("one of the burning issues of the day"). The Sunday opening of museums and art galleries gained growing support, and Sabbatarianism and the Lord's Day Observance Society remained prime targets. Change in leisure activities on Sunday would take people from secularist meetings as well as churches, as was recognised when it was admitted that Sunday entertainment would "draw a lot of strength from our part". New patterns of leisure were to make greater inroads on Sunday than the cries of the secularists, as was implied in an article on "Bicycles and Religion": "Not even attractive church services can hold a candle against sunlight and sweet scenery, and so the bicycle, even in Sabbatarian Scotland, is becoming the great agency for rationalizing the day which the men of God have claimed for their master—that is to say, for themselves." (12 July, 1896.)

The *Freethinker* recommended cremation to freethinkers, regarding burial as a Christian superstition. The Home Secretary, Sir William Harcourt, was roundly condemned for opposing cremation as "repugnant to the general feelings of the community". (The *Freethinker* had an elephantine memory for its old enemies and Sir William Harcourt, Home Secretary during the blasphemy trial and imprisonment of Foote was given a scathing obituary: "Twenty-one years ago he did us grievous wrong. And he did it meanly." (13 March, 1904.) The particular complaint was his calumny that Foote was gaoled for obscenity — "a mean and infamous lie about us" — but the failure to respond to Memorials to mitigate the blasphemy sentences must have left a legacy of bitterness.).

Freedom and Sexuality

Freethinkers were in the lead in championing birth control, discussing women's rights, and examining matters of sexual morality. Foote personally supported the Malthusian League and availability of contraceptive facilities, but the *Freethinker* did not include birth control propaganda. There were advertisements such as "Advice to the Married — 'Prudence and Plenty' plus list of modern appliances from Manufacturers of Hygienic and Malthusian Appliances." Even that was controversial and a debate took place in the *Agnostic Journal* over whether the *Freethinker* should carry advertisements for contraceptives. (1892, passim.)

The Knowlton trial had shown that birth control could be controversial amongst freethinkers. The association between contraception, free love and free thought was one which secularists were anxious to avoid. Although most secularists seem to have lived lives of almost monotonous propriety, there was a practical connection between contraception and free love, and those who wished to break sexual taboos often also wished to puncture repressive religious morality. The sensitiveness of secularists to accusations of immorality was due to the extent to which false attacks were made to smear and belittle freethinkers' lives and ideas.

Birth control was associated by its proponents, like Annie Besant, with the right of women to organise their own lives and to participate in society in ways other than perpetual child-bearing. Foote and the *Freethinker* were somewhat ambivalent in their attitude to women. They saw the justness of giving women greater possibilities, and recognised the part of Christianity in promoting a submissive ideal of womanhood, but feared that women were more religious and less radical than men. Foote wrote: "Michelet said truly of religions, that they are born and they die on the bosom of woman." (4 May, 1884.) He also said in an article on "Jesus on Women" that "Women are everywhere the chief, and in some places the only, supporters of religion." But he also referred to J.S. Mill's "great essay" on "The Subjection of Women" and "Shelley's great cry

'Can man be free if woman be a slave?' " and saw "the great hope of the future" in "the education and elevation of women." (19 September, 1886.)

The *Freethinker* could be scathing about the Biblical attitude to women: "The Tenth Commandment makes her domestic property, and Paul winds up by telling her that her sole duty is to play second fiddle in a minor key." W.P. Ball revised St. Paul's injunction in a skit in which St. Paulina calls for "the man to learn in silence and with all subjection."

Foote defended marriage against the "new woman" in a front-page review of Grant Allen's didactic novel *The Women Who Did*, but in reasoned and not reproving tones:

> We are not of those who use the phrase 'free love' as a reproach, for love was never anything else but free. It cannot be commanded. It cannot be had to order. It is spontaneous, like all our affections. Nevertheless, the freedom, not of feeling, but of action, which Mr. Grant Allen pleads for, runs dangerously near to promiscuity; or at least to an instability that is almost as bad. (3 March, 1895.)

In arguing for marriage for the sake of children, he claimed "Rights must be balanced by duties". However, an article on the "New Woman" by the pseudonymous "Uncle Benjamin" said of the "new woman": "She merely is not ashamed of her sex, and holds that the same code of morality should apply to men and to women." (7 April, 1895.) And an article "The Gospel of Happiness" by Frederick Ryan discussed Grant Allen's essay "The New Hedonism" in the *Fortnightly*, responding favourably to his attack on Christian ascetisim and self-sacrifice. "Self-development is greater than self-sacrifice" was an epigram of Grant Allen which would have appealed to freethinkers, but in the last decade of the century when Victorian prudery and hypocrisy were challenged by major figures like Havelock Ellis, Shaw, Ibsen, and Edward Carpenter, the *Freethinker* approached sexual morality with the caution of a middle-aged radical.

The Legitimation League founded in 1893 to campaign for legal rights for illegitimate children was at first linked closely with secularism, but as it became more extreme and advocated co-habitation without marriage a rift with secularists arose. The prosecution of the secretary of the Legitimation League, George Bedborough, for selling a copy of *Sexual Inversion* by Havelock Ellis was an important case. The *Freethinker* was not a pioneer in arguing for the rights of homosexuals; the Bible's mention of sodomy was used as an example of its immorality and unsuitability for children, and there was no mention of the Oscar Wilde trial in 1895. The Bedborough case looked like becoming a test case for free speech, and a Free Press Defence Committee was formed, the members of which included Grant Allen, Shaw, Carpenter and Foote, Holyoake and Robertson. But Bedborough's plea of guilty and secret deal with the police to end the Legitimation League caused a collapse of the free speech case and the last decade of the century ended with no major breakthrough in sexual law reform or free speech. [1])

Another issue of sexual morality given much prominence in the 80s and 90s was prostitution. W.T. Stead's campaign against child prostitution in the *Pall Mall Gazette* stired the press, the churches and the politicians into a frenzy of self-righteousness, which did not impress Foote. He noted that Stead included obscene details which made his paper sell spectacularly well: "It is astonishing what an itch there is among the chaste Christian public for surreptitious sexual excitement." (19 July, 1884.). The following week he said priests who denounce the abominable debauchery of young girls "are the grossest hypocrites, when, at the same time, they place the Bible in the hands of English maidens."

Foote did not support prostitution, but he said it would never be stamped out and believed "A woman is forced into prostitution by economical causes." (28 October, 1894.) The *Freethinker* was sceptical towards "fanatics of purity" — "and especially of *compulsory* purity". An article headed "Living Pictures" gives a fair impression of the *Freethinker*'s attitude towards morality campaigners and prostitution. Mr. William Coote of the National Vigilance Association had complained to the Licensing Committee of the London County Council about certain Tableaux Vivants, or Living Pictures, because some of the figures appeared naked, as a result of costumes resembling "a kind of skin". Foote retorted: "It would not be surprising if he got up a petition to the Creator to bring us all into the world with an irremovable covering, which might expand with our growth, like the garments of the Jews in the wilderness... The nude in itself is not indecent... A lifted skirt, the artful gleam of a mere inch of threat, the pose of the body, a glance of the eyes, may be infinitely suggestive..." Mrs. Ormiston Chant had objected to promenades at the Empire, where immoral women were allowed to perambulate. Foote reports that an interviewer said the woman had done nothing "in the way of their Trade" "beyond the elevation of an eyebrow or the use of an impudent look... Fancy a committee of Mrs. Chants inspecting the music-halls, and bringing a woman before the magistrates for wearing an impudent look — as a woman is apt to do when another woman stares at her." (28 October, 1894.)

The *Freethinker* objected to the censorship of books which dealt more explicitly with sexual matters than hitherto in the century. The English publisher of Zola's works, Vizetelly, was prosecuted at the instance of the National Vigilance Association and sentenced to three months in gaol. *Madame Bovary's* publication led to a similar prosecution. Foote commented that the publishers of the Bible should also be prosecuted. In a piece provoked by Tennyson's reference in his long poem *Locksley Hall* to the "troughs of Zolaism", Foote wrote: "The 'Zolaism' of the Bible is far more pernicious than the 'Zolaism' of French fiction." (19 December, 1886.)

[1]) See Arthur Calder-Marshall: *Lewd, Blasphemous and Obscene* for the full story.

Any attempts to prevent the sale of the *Freethinker* naturally led to vigorous opposition. In 1885 the case of a Scottish bookseller, Robert Ferguson, sentenced to 14 days' imprisonment under a charge of selling profane illustrations in the *Freethinker* under the Glasgow Police Act of 1866 led to a flurry of protest. The case was dropped at an Appeal Court, but it apparently worried other booksellers enough to reduce circulation.

Morality and Progressive Causes

In matters of individual morality, sexuality, and censorship, reciprocity and the golden rule were seen as the basis of behaviour. In an article which is sceptical of the over-academic approach of a symposium in the *Agnostic Annual,* Foote examined the question "Why live a moral life?" and placed considerable emphasis upon the feelings:

> Morality is not based upon logic, but upon feeling. Thinking discovers consequences, but it does not discriminate them. Reason shows us how to reach our object, but feeling decides what object we try to reach. The recognition of this truth is essential to ethical progress. We talk a great deal about education in these days, but the education of the feelings is curiously neglected. Five minutes attention to this matter is worthy a hundred years of argument on the question, 'Why live a moral life?' Some day or other, when we have got over this squabble about religion in our public schools, we shall give children moral training instead of dosing them with wise saws and maxims. Their senses and imaginations will be appealed to by music, by works of art, by the vital history of great men and the great things that have been done in the world. Lessons of this kind will sink into them and insensibly mould their lives. (11 November, 1894.)

Education was a topic that constantly occurred in the *Freethinker* (especially during the early years of the twentieth century). The School Boards which were established by the 1870 Education Act gave opportunities for the election of secularists to school boards. Aveling was briefly on the important London board, and the *Freethinker* sometimes urged readers to work for the election of secularists, but churchmen were much more powerful and efficient in this respect and the school boards were dominated by religious interests. The argument about how much Bible instruction should be given was lost through lack of influence. There was disagreement among secularists as to whether to completely remove the Bible and religious topics from schools or whether to give "an education inspired by Humanity's entire story — a story which includes the Bible and all other expressions of the genius of our race" as F.J. Gould and the Moral Instruction League wanted. J.M. Wheeler thought a completely free secular education should be financed by the disestablishment of the Church of England. There was not just the wrangle over secular and religious education, but a deep belief in the value of education as a means of progress for humanity: "Let us starve the priest and plump the schoolmasters; let us cease telling people to be good and train them to be useful." (24 October, 1886.)

Foote took an interest in a range of progressive causes. Like many ex-prisoners, he was very concerned with prison reform and spoke to the Humanitarian League on the subject. Foote moved a motion proposing "That... the idea of reform should be substituted for that of punishment in the treatment of criminals, so that gaols may no longer be places of brutalisation, or even detention, but places of physical, intellectual and moral elevation for those afflicted with anti-social tendencies." (10 March, 1895.) It was seconded by Shaw.

On another occasion Foote gave the Humanitarian League a lecture entitled "The Kinship of Life. — A Secularist's View of Animal Rights." It appears remarkably advanced in presenting an ecological view of the interrelatedness of all life:

> Darwin and his successors have demonstrated the kinship of life, and thus the lowliest of organisms that swim, or creep, or fly, or run, are brought — at first negatively, and then positively — within the scope of the spirit of brotherhood...
>
> ...It is enough to make a decent person sick to read of the agony inflicted by 'sportsmen' on helpless rabbits, pigeons, pheasants, and deer.
>
> ...With regard to the Food Question, I admit the progress of Vegetarianism, but it will take a long time to wean the majority from flesh-eating; ... I am a vegetarian myself, but I take a little meat with it. Let us deal with the existing situation... I am strongly in favour of the most drastic regulation of the slaughter-house and the cattle-ship.
>
> ...I regard it [Vivisection] as the ultimate horror of man's unjust dealing with the animals. I believe that Secularists are prepared to support legislation for its entire prohibition... When an anarchist told me, soon after the assassination of President Carnot, that new ideas had their baptism in blood, I told him that I did not object to their shedding blood: they might shed all they had; what I objected to was their shedding the blood of others. If some person full of scientific zeal, and burning with the enthusiasm of humanity, will offer himself to be vivisected, I shall respect his generosity, whatever I may think of his intelligence. But I object to his offering me. He must wait till I offer myself. And I object to his offering any other man — or any other animal.
>
> Let us be humane to each other, and the spirit of humanity will naturally extend itself to the whole kinship of life. (6, 13 March, 1904.)

The *Freethinker* regularly reported the International Congress of Freethought and the issues it debated. (There were frequent motions opposing the persecution of Jews and all persecution for matters of belief.) An international contact which made a strong impression on Foote was his visit to America in 1896. He sent back vivid letters for publication in the *Freethinker.* He lectured to American freethought audiences. The event which most excited him was his meeting with Ingersoll and his family: "There is something in Shakespeare to make mountains look little, and there is something in Ingersoll to make the busy streets of New York look trivial."

Freethinker Contributors

Although a large proportion of the *Freethinker* was written by Foote in its first thirty years, there were other important regular contributors. J.M. Wheeler was Foote's closest friend and was sub-editor until his death in 1898. He shared Foote's love of literature and wrote many of the most scholarly historical articles in the *Freethinker.* He wrote a sketch of a history of Freethought in the *Freethinker* (1897, reprinted in *An Anthology of Atheism and Rationalism,* ed. by G. Stein, Prometheus Books, 1980) which concluded:

> Freethinkers have stood in the vanguard of progress, fronting the fire of the enemy, and sheltering behind their backs all the feebler fry. They have taken the danger, the antipathy, and the odium, while behind them even the Protestant Church has advanced some measure of freedom. The day is not now one for giants only, but for each one doing his level best to leave the world better than he found it.

Unfortunately he was prone to breakdowns and mania, but his studiousness and gentleness were admired by all — even the secretary of the Christian Evidence Society sent a letter of condolence when he died.

Joseph Symes contributed many articles in the first few years of the *Freethinker.* He wrote a regular Atheist's Sermon. He moved to Melbourne in 1884, where he founded his own journal and devoted much of his life to spreading freethought in Australia. [1]

Charles Watts (1836-1906) wrote many articles for the *Freethinker* in the 1890s. He was the first Secretary of the N.S.S., and a staunch colleague of Bradlaugh. His decision not to support the republication of *The Fruits of Philosophy* in 1877 led to a permanent rift. In 1884 he went to Toronto where he worked for freethought until 1891. On his return to England he became an N.S.S. vice-president and a regular contributor to the *Freethinker.* He fell out with Foote a few years before his death, when it was believed he was showing greater loyalty to the Rationalist Press Association (founded by his son Charles Albert Watts.)

Arthur B. Moss (1855-1937) was a very longstanding writer for the *Freethinker,* producing 321 articles between 1883 and 1934 (Taylor: *Chronology of Freethought*). He was an energetic outdoor lecturer, a freelance journalist, and active in local politics in South London where he was a pillar of the Camberwell Secular Society.

By the turn of the century Chapman Cohen had become a contributor to the *Freethinker.* He wrote "The Religious Outlook" for the issue of 7 January, 1900, in which he looked back at the great period of the *Freethinker's* first twenty years and forward to the *Freethinker's* role in the coming century — a role to which his own contribution was to be crucial:

> 'The wonderful Century' is rapidly nearing its close. It has been a period replete with new ideas filled with burning enthusiasms, witnessing many

[1] See pamphlets by Nigel Sinnott about Joseph Symes.

drastic and far-reaching reforms, and bids fair to close its career with the promise of still more startling changes in the immediate future. Like a stone gathering momentum in its fall to the earth, the certainty and directness of Progress became greater as the knowledge of man increased with the labour of each passing generation. A child to-day is born the possessor of an intellectual heritage that would have formed the stock-in-trade of a philosopher thirty centuries ago. Slowly but certainly Nature yields up her secrets to patient investigation; the miraculous is lost in the wonders daily disclosed by science; the prophet gives place to the professor, the priest to the sociologist, the search for God's will to the study of man's nature and legitimate needs.

Great as the changes have been in all departments of thought, they have been nowhere greater than in the field of religion. Complete freedom of expression has not been quite secured, but the majority are ashamed of being credited with bigotry; and, when people resent as an insult the imputation of being possessors of a particular frame of mind, they have taken the first step towards getting rid of it altogether. Civil equality and political rights are no longer wholly a question of religious opinion. Christians and Jews, Deists and Atheists, meet on equal terms upon the platform of common citizenship, and this, again is a good sign — for Freethought...

So far as the fundamental ideas of religion are concerned, the changes have been still more sweeping. Here it is not too much to say that the whole current conception of religion has undergone a profound and radical alteration. Quite apart from the development of Biblical criticism, which has completely dissolved the views of the Bible that were current when the century opened, the enormous expansion of science, both theoretical and applied, with the growth of sociology, have combined to produce a frame of mind to which fundamental religious ideas are altogether alien. The nature of religious ideas is no longer shrouded in the mystery that formed their chief protection and recommendation. Anthropology has taught us the fashion of their birth, and, in so doing, has quite certainly indicated the manner of their ultimate death...

And now what of the future? Whatever may be the rate of progress in the immediate future, we may safely reckon upon the continued operation of the same forces as in the past. On the one side, we shall have a set of half-obsolete rules, in which the supernatural will become less and less evident but upon the acceptance of which the social status of the clergy will depend, and to secure acceptance of which they will stick at little...

On the other side we can safely count upon the continued operation of different social and economic forces that will do much to weaken the power of religion, and not a little to destroy it altogether. And these are not to be despised. Christianity's deadliest enemies are often not found among logical and scientific proofs of its falsity so much as among different lines of social development, which, by broadening the mind and directing attention to the essential conditions of social welfare, destroy the particular type of intellect on which religion lives. Thousands of people who never think of listening to a direct attack on religious ideas find their beliefs slipping away from them through causes they are altogether unable to understand. They know their religion goes; they know not the manner of its going. And beyond these forces there is the great principle of independent religious criticism which it is our chief task to promote. This should certainly not become weaker as time advances... On the contrary... We of the Secular Societies exist to bring this about. It is our task to lead the direct attack on the fortress of religion, to point out the bearings of social and scientific developments on religious beliefs and the conclusions to be drawn therefrom, to direct into more useful channels the energy at present squandered on religion, and it is the duty of all who value intellectual uprightness and social well-being to help in the work. (7 January, 1900.)

CHAPTER III
FOOTE AND COHEN IN HARNESS IN THE TWENTIETH CENTURY

Chapman Cohen adopted a less aggressive attack on Christianity and saw its decline as a sociological fact to be coolly analysed. This made him none the less determined in his belief in secularist principles and his exposure of the myths and morality of Christianity. His calm persistence kept him writing for the *Freethinker* from 1897 to 1951, as editor from 1915 — a remarkable journalistic achievement by any standards.

Cohen was born in 1868 in Leicester of a Jewish family which had lived in England for over two hundred years. His upbringing was not in the least religious: there were certain religious ceremonies in his home but "they cannot have made any particular impression on me". He was withdrawn from religious instruction at school. Unlike most freethinkers, therefore, he underwent no rejection of religion, with the anger and pain sometimes involved. "In my own case I had no pains in giving up religion. In sober truth I cannot recall a time when I had any religion to give up." *(Almost An Autobiography.* A collection of articles and some biographical details spun together when he was 71.) Where Foote's chief interests had been literary, Cohen's concerns were more philosophical: "... in the main I think I read more for ideas and he more for the pure love of good writing." He was a prodigious reader as a youngster, moving from boys' tales to the standard novelists and then history, science and philosophy. "...I can definitely date the fact that before I was eighteen I was familiar with Spinoza, Locke, Hume and Berkeley, besides having revelled in the Platonic dialogues, a love for which I have never outgrown." He claimed that Spinoza and Herbert Spencer were his greatest teachers. It was a different background from the radicalism of Paine or the fierce anti-religion of Carlile; Cohen was pleased to see himself "examining the different forms of religious belief with the same detached curiosity that a Professor of Zoology would study and classify specimens in a museum."

This voracious reader was thrown into the public arena of controversy and campaigns by chance. In the summer of 1889 he stopped to listen to a Christian Evidence Society speaker in Victoria Park. The Christian Evidence Society speaker was opposed by an old gentleman with a speech imediment, and when more opposition was invited Cohen attacked the speaker for his ridicule of the old man's speech impediment and "received much applause from the crowd."

> A week or so later I was again listening to the same speaker, and at his invitation I again spoke twice — in opposition. The next thing was I received an invitation from the local Branch to give a lecture or two on the Secular Society's platform. I consented, and have been lecturing from that platform ever since.

Cohen's personal life was uneventful and he claimed that he sought excitement in adventures of the mind. "My home life has been so free from trouble or serious discordance, that it would be quite uninteresting to outsiders." He wrote warmly of his marriage and of friendship, and in a rare mention of personal sorrow referred to the death of his daughter, aged 29, commenting philosophically: "The dead do not suffer, grief is part of the price we pay for affection."

In later life he regretted that he had not started writing earlier. He wrote for other papers before the *Freethinker* and was briefly editor of the Bradford *Truthseeker* (later to be owned by J.W. Gott) while the then editor, John Grange, was ill. Foote had frequently asked him to write for the *Freethinker*, "but I did no more than write accounts of my lecture tours." However, early reluctance soon gave way to prolific persistence: and an "occasional article" in 1897 soon became a regular piece, and after the death of Wheeler in 1898 he assisted with sub-editing, taking an increasingly important role, sometimes bearing the main burden when Foote was ill, until he succeeded Foote as editor on his death in 1915.

Secular Education

The last fifteen years of Foote's editorship continued in what had become a steady and familiar vein. As society was becoming broadly secularised, the *Freethinker* concentrated upon key points in the transition — upon the struggle for secular education, which was a substantial party political issue in England and provided a freethought martyr, Ferrer, in Spain. The conflict between Catholics and anti-clericals over laicisation in France was of major interest. Issues such as imperialism, war, blasphemy, censorship, strikes and suffragettes continued to draw what Foote thought of as "non-political" comment. The hammering of religion, whether the old fundamentalists or new theologians, began to look repetitive; articles were reprinted, but they came afresh to new readers. There was a consistent emphasis on reciprocal morality and secularist principles.

Freethinkers saw the struggle between church and chapel to dominate schools as an opportunity to press for entirely secular education. Although secular education was pressed hard by freethinkers and gained the support of MPs and the Trades Union Council, by 1914 the opportunity had clearly been lost. Balfour's Education Act of 1902, which did much to further secondary education, was seen by Non-Conformists to favour Anglicans and there was an outcry against it. Passive resisters led by Dr. Clifford, who became an arch-fiend in the eyes of the *Freethinker*, refused to pay rates. G.J. Holyoake, who was friendly with Dr. Clifford, joined them in passive resistance and the *Freethinker's* longstanding antipathy towards him was given new impetus.

The so-called "Non-Conformist conscience" was prominent in the 1906 election and the Liberal landslide was seen by the *Freethinker* as a capitulation to the Non-Conformists. Foote wrote at the time of the impending election: "Non-Conformists are as determined as ever in making education the occasion of securing a mere sectarian victory over the Established Church; the only interest of Freethinkers in the situation is in how far it may become the means of expelling religious instruction from the schools altogether." (7 January, 1906.) An Education Bill brought in by Mr. Birrell, after the election, was castigated on the front page of the *Freethinker:*

> It should not be called an Education Bill. There is nothing in it about education... The whole and sole object of the Bill is the re-arrangement of educational machinery in the interest of the religious faction which boasts having "got its own back" at the recent general election. (29 April, 1906.)

The *Freethinker* particularly objected to the use of the Bible in school. Writing of the Education Bill, Foote declared the Protestant Bible was "set up as a fetish in elementary schools." Just as Christians were divided in their attitude to religion in schools, so freethinkers also had their differences. Charles Watts thought that the Bible should remain as part of children's education so that they knew what religion was about and because "It is the hardest thing in the world to convert a 'nothingarian' to Freethought." (6 November, 1887.) (A parallel argument comes from some freethinkers today, who say that school assemblies and RE are valuable in putting children off religion for life — but the logic is cynical.)

Freethinkers were divided into those who wanted religion kept out of schools entirely and those who wanted broad teaching about morality, religion and humanity.The *Freethinker* and Foote usually took the former line, but a Moral Instruction League was founded in 1898 at a public meeting in which the N.S.S., the Freethought Federation, the I.L.P. and other radical and ethical organisations took part. F.J. Gould was a vigorous proponent of "an Education inspired by Humanity's entire story — a story which includes the Bible and all other expressions of the genius of the race." (F.J. Gould's occasional "ethical sermons" were a colourful feature of the *Freethinker* during this period and indicate that its columns embraced a wide spectrum of the views of those whom Gould was already referring to as "us Humanists" as early as 1909 in an article proposing that "It is the highest maximum of the Religion of Humanity to live for others.")

A clause in the 1906 Education Bill that made only secular education compulsory, so that rather than opting out of an individual lesson children need not attend school at all for any religious aspect, was lost in the House of Lords. Foote wrote that "The Bishops — who are absent when a Bill to prevent pigeon shooting is before the House — have turned up in full force when they see a chance of forcing their religion down the throats of children whose parents regard it with mingled feelings of disgust and contempt." (25 November, 1906.) The whole Bill was eventually lost — a triumph for the Anglican Bishops over the "Nonconformist conscience".

The Secular Education League was founded in 1907 as a result of the failure of the Bill and the secularists Foote, Joseph McCabe and Hypatia Bradlaugh Bonner were on the committee. Despite the support of some Labour MPs it had no impact on legislation or the educational system. (See R.S.R. Royle, p 309-316.)

France and Spain

The *Freethinker* paid considerable attention to the disestablishment of the Catholic Church in France. Foote was interested in French history and literature and felt the French anti-clerical tradition could set an example for Europe. When the Dreyfus affair eventually concluded with Dreyfus's release from prison in 1906, Foote praised the atheist Zola, for playing a crucial part in uncovering injustice by writing "J'accuse" and reported a speech given by Anatole France at a demonstration by the League of the Rights of Man at the tomb of Zola. The Separation of Church and State which the French government effected between 1905 and 1906, caused a shriek of pain and defiance from Pope Pius X and bitter quarrels between Catholics and Protestants. The *Freethinker* was emphatic that freethinkers should not emulate the intolerance of Catholics:

> It is particularly unworthy of M. Clemenceau and M. Briand, who are outspoken Freethinkers. Being such they should act more wisely and considerately towards Catholics than Catholics have acted towards Freethinkers. What are our principles worth if they allow us to imitate the bad example of our enemies? We ought to be true to *our own* principles. (2 December, 1906.)

An article on "The Pope's Grievances" showed some sympathy for the Catholic Church's plight, especially for the loss of wealth which they were compelled to hand over to lay committees: "In reality it is the kidnapping of the clergy by the State..." (15 April, 1906.)

There was the same opposition to Protestant intolerance of Catholics when sectarian violence broke out in Liverpool in 1909. Foote wrote firmly:

> Mob violence should not be tolerated for a moment in a civilised community... It makes no difference whether Protestants attack Catholics or Catholics attack Protestants, or both attack Freethinkers... We would protect the Liverpool Catholics at all costs, just as we would protect Protestants, Jews, Freethinkers, or any other denomination. (19 September, 1909.)

But there was a caveat about Catholics who "plead for toleration when they are in the minority and practice intolerance when they are in the majority" and a reference to the execution of Francisco Ferrer in Spain.

The case of Ferrer was referred to in the *Freethinker* in great detail. Francisco Ferrer was a pioneer of secular education and an active anarchist in Spain, who was accused of playing a key part in a rebellion, imprisoned for a year, tried by court martial and found guilty on insubstantial and (according to later investigators) trumped-up evidence.

He was executed by firing squad. Freethinkers assumed he was framed by the Catholic Church, being "hated by the all-powerful clergy 'because he is spending the whole of his fortune building popular rationalist schools in Spain.' " (22 August, 1909.) After the execution, Foote proposed a motion at a large public meeting at St. James's Hall, London, to condemn one of "the worst of modern atrocities". The motion concluded by rejoicing that "the act of his murderers has raised a storm of indignation throughout the civilised world."

Foote's speech was reported in the *Freethinker:*

> ...The rifle-shots that were heard in the moat of the fortress of Montjuich have reverberated throughout Europe. (Applause.)
>
> Ferrer has been slain by the Spain of the Inquisition, the Spain of Torquemada and Cortes, the Spain of Alava and the bloody massacres and cruelties of the Netherlands, the Spain of the expulsion of the Jews, the Spain of the expulsion of the Moors...
>
> Ferrer is a martyr. (Hear, hear) We know very well what his crime was. He tried to make people think (hear, hear); he knew that education was the only way to do that (applause), and educationists are never practisers of violence. (Applause.) A man who goes in for education goes in for the slow but sure method. Education is the most terrible of all dynamite (hear, hear) when applied to tyranny, superstition, and inhumanity.
>
> Ferrer died as a Freethinker. After compassing his death in the name of religion — for that is what it means (Applause),— they had the disgusting hypocrisy to press their pious attentions upon his last hours. They actually wanted him to kiss the crucifix! They wanted Giordano Bruno to do that, and in those days they made it red hot! Ferrer kissed no crucifix, and listened to no priest, but met his death like a man. (Applause.) (24 October, 1909.)

Concern with the case continued with a reprint of Dr. Simarro's article "The Ferrer Case and European Opinion", which examined the judicial aspects of the affair (19 February, 1911) and a report of the inauguration of a monument to Ferrer in Brussels by William Heaford, who represented the N.S.S. on the occasion. (19 November, 1911.)

A comparison between Spain and Portugal contained praise for Dr. Brago, who brought in a Constitutional Republic: "No lover of God — for he is an Atheist, but a lover of his fellowmen, he has shown (as Ferrer did in Spain) with what noble serenity Atheists can face the heaviest tasks and sternest duties." (3 September, 1911.)

In commenting on international affairs the *Freethinker* continued to question imperialism and the arrogance of missionaries who imposed European life-styles and an alien religion upon other countries. Gould, in an article entitled "The Alien Goat", ridiculed the introduction of the frock coat and tall hat into Liberia and quoted Nansen's book on *Eskimo Life* in which the arctic explorer asserts that "it would be better for Greenland if Christianity had never been carried to the romantic 'icy mountains' of which Bishop Heber has taught us to sing so ignorantly and absurdly." (24 January, 1909.) There was a sarcastic reference to Mr. Joynson-Hicks, later to gain notoriety as the moral crusader and

Home Secretary, 'Jix'; he said in a political speech in Manchester "we conquered India as an outlet for the goods of Great Britain" and the *Freethinker* retorted "—What a glorious mixture of ambition, rapacity and religion!" (19 December, 1909.)

Another politician whose early career was observed with asperity was Winston Churchill. (The *Freethinker* was unlikely to be well-disposed towards the son of Randolph Churchill, who had played a prominent part in opposing Bradlaugh's entry into Parliament.) Electioneering in Manchester in 1906, Churchill visited a "Ragged-school", asked for a "Glory Song" and said it had "deeply touched him and lifted him into a serene region above the brutal details of politics and elections. "Well," it was written in the *Freethinker,* "we hope this was only a bit of blarney. We should be sorry to think that the 'Glory Song' was Mr. Churchill's idea of either music or poetry."

Social Reform

In the wider political field G.W. Foote maintained a tangential, "non-political" stance. His view that ideas are more important than votes was confirmed in an earlier suggestion of the justice of proportional representation. Foote pointed out in an Acid Drop that the 1906 election showed a discrepancy between the proportion of overall votes and the proportion of Liberal, Conservative and Labour MPs; he also remarked that "In the long run, it is not polling and numbers but truth and logic that win the day." (28 January, 1906.)

The suffragette question gained surprisingly little prominence, despite a general belief in the importance of women's contribution to freethought: "And if the Freethought husband can make his wife a Freethinker, he will make his children Freethinkers too." (5 March, 1911.) Foote criticised the break-up of a public meeting by suffragettes. The meeting was to be addressed by Mr. Cremer, MP, on "Peace and Arbitration", and Cremer had opposed women's suffrage in the House of Commons. Foote's comment was confined to the "Ethics of Public Meetings" and avoided commitment to votes for women (25 November, 1906.)

An article, "Women and Freethought", in the same month justified the *Freethinker's* position and accurately propounded the freethought outlook:

> Attempts were made, many years ago, to drive the Freethought party into adoption of Socialism. This was met by attempts to drive it into the adoption of Individualism. Both efforts were mistaken, and the success of either would have been disastrous. The Freethought party would have been divided at once; some other effort would have been made to commit it to something else, which would have caused another division, and the last two members would have eventually wished each other good-bye.
>
> Freethought in relation to politics and sociology is not a dogma; it can never be more than an attitude... Freethinkers cannot be expected to see

> eye to eye with each other in relation to the vast variety of questions that have to be settled in civilised communities. Differences of capacity, temperament, training and knowledge will naturally assert themselves. All we have a right to expect is that Freethinkers will be more reasonable, and consequently more humane, than their superstitious fellow citizens.
>
> Freethinkers who differ...[share] a faith in human reason and an enthusiasm for human welfare. (11 November, 1906.)

On the more specific issues of health and welfare the *Freethinker* preferred social reform to soup kitchens and Charles Watts asked in an article on "Health and Poverty": "What has Christianity, as such, done to remove the appalling evils of poverty?" (1 April, 1900.) A similar view was expressed in an Acid Drop: "Some of the clergy are advocating the use of prayer as a preventive against small-pox. They might as well try to tempt an earthquake with a hot-cross-bun." (12 March, 1911.)

The Church Army and General Booth continued as butts of G.W. Foote, because of their soup-kitchen approach. King Edward VII was criticised for supporting the Church Army and the *Freethinker* suggested "leaving religious philanthropists alone — for they are all based on false economics and labor sweating. His Majesty would do infinitely more good by helping along the policy of Old Age Pensions for the workers..." (25 February, 1906.)

The monarchy remained unpopular in the *Freethinker* columns and the Coronation of George V was criticised for its expense and as "A Carnival of Cant". The nub of opposition to the monarchy lay in the traditional freethought analysis of an alliance of kingcraft and priest-craft:

> The ceremony is symbolical of the supremacy of the Church or of religion in secular life. But, again, who believes in this being the case?
>
> ...Yet it is not without significance this alliance of religion with certain social ceremonies and institutions. Privilege and piety belong to the same culture stage of human history. Religion lives on credulity, and cupidity fattens both. If the people are to be exploited they must first of all be befooled; and every appeal to the barbaric and slavish instincts in human nature are means to this end...(9 July, 1911.)

Foote bemoaned the "people befooled", but the people in rebellion were also criticised. Widespread strikes in 1911 led to outbreaks of violence and looting. The *Freethinker* was stern about indiscipline and drew lessons about the evil of religion and the development of individual morality rather than the impact of class divisions. Wales was a scene of disorder and Foote wrote:

> South Wales is inhabited by too many people who are full of religion and beer. The riots there during the railway strike were the worst in the whole country. The rioters did not fight for Trade Unionism but for loot...
>
> ...England, who sends out missionaries to the well-behaved heathen, has within her own borders a large hooligan population who delight in disorder, looting and arson. Let her attend to her own goths and vandals before trying to 'civilise' distant countries.

An article about "God and the Strikers" wondered how the clergy would use the strike to show the beneficent influence of Christianity:

> Two thousand years after Christ there is no love lost among Christians. Self-love is rampant. Every side in industrial quarrels talks of "*our* rights" and "*your* duties". The idea of a moral obligation binding on all for the good of all scarcely exists. You may find it in Marcus Aurelius and Epictetus — one an emperor the other a slave, of sixteen hundred years ago, and both Pagans — but not in the political and social controversies of today. Yet nothing else will ever save a nation. The idea that civilisation can be evolved out of the painfully adjusted clash of mere self-interests — whether of the classes or the masses — is one of the saddest of modern fallacies. (27 August, 1911.)

Moral Obligations

An emphasis on moral obligation, present even in the early strident days, has always been contained in the *Freethinker.* A typical flavour of moral endeavour is caught in Charles Watts' answer to the perennial question of what do you put in the place of Christianity ("A Substitute for Christianity"):

> I would substitute for dependence upon religious faith, the reliance upon cultivated reason; for the providence of heaven, the science of earth; for the divine commands, ethical teachings; for prayer, work; for worship in churches, inculcation of secular truths; for ministers of religion, political and social reforms; and, finally, instead of the useless efforts of preparing for some imaginary future life, I would urge the necessity of persistent striving to better our present existence.
>
> ...As Secularists, we have no heaven in another world to allure, no hell to appal, and no devil to torture. We urge that it is far better to seek to realise a real "heaven on earth", and to get rid of those shams and superstitions which too often make a "hell upon earth". We teach that vice should be avoided because indulgence in it is a wrong to individuals and to society, and that virtue should be practised because it is the duty of all to do what is possible to alleviate human woe and to assist human progress. (2 December, 1900.)

Individual striving may seem a meek alternative to revolutionary programmes, but freethinkers honestly believe that the human lot may be ameliorated more by reform and individual effort than turning the world upside down. This can lead to a naive belief that human behaviour is easily changed, as for instance in the article "Secularism at Work" by the ex-Presbyterian minister, who wrote regularly for the *Freethinker,* John Lloyd:

> What is needed is an instructed reason to supply healthy training for the emotions, and this we shall not secure, on any large scale, until our system of education has been completely reconstructed on strictly secular lines. Morality is an affair of the world alone... There can be no high morality without good physical health. All anti-social tendencies and activities are the outcome of disease. (3 December, 1911.)

Lloyd does not always betray such simple-minded ideas, but he rarely loses the tone of a preacher in exhorting a secular morality:

> Secularism calls on men to believe in and trust themselves. Self-reliance engenders self-respect, and self-respect develops self-balance, which is self-harmony... The standard of morality is within, and our privilege is to rise to it and bring it to the surface of our being, so that it may permeate us through and through. ("Secularism and Morality", 10 January, 1902.)

Chapman Cohen consistently made the crucial point that morality is not related to religion: "In its earlier stages religion is non-moral..." Religion was, in his view, related to fear: "Religion is essentially a theory that exists to explain a given set of phenomena. Morality, on the other hand, takes its rise in those feelings and instincts that are developed in human and animal nature by the struggle for existence." (5 September, 1909.)

The assault on religion was always combined, in Cohen's mind, with an attempt to explain it as a social and historical phenomenon. He was unhappy with a description of religion, such as Matthew Arnold's, as "morality touched with emotion", because "A definition that covers everything may, for all the good it does, as well not cover anything." (5 September, 1909.) The writings of anthropologists and historians were used to demolish new theologians as well as fundamentalist Christians. Three key works are referred to in John Lloyd's questions, hurled at modern theologians, in his article "The Dilemma of Modern Theology": "... who, among them all, has answered Mr. Frazer's *Golden Bough*, or Mr. Robertson's *Pagan Christs*? Who, among them all, can explain away the hundreds of facts cited in Mr. Grant Allen's *Evolution of the Idea of God*?" (17 January, 1902.)

The Freethinker and Bernard Shaw

Ideas of evolution and god, in a different sense, were prominent in an argument between Shaw and Foote in the pages of the *Freethinker*. The *Freethinker* had an edgy relationship with Shaw. GBS had briefly participated at secularist meetings in the 1880s, but concentrated upon Fabianism and other fields. The *Freethinker* admired his trenchant criticism of Christianity and opposition to Blasphemy Law, but disliked his criticism of secularists and enthusiasm for the "life-force". An open letter to the *Freethinker*, headed "Mr. Bernard Shaw Explains His Religion" was published on the front page. Shaw asked why he was regarded by so many secularists as an apostate:

> The answer is that I am contemptuously and implacably anti-rationalist and anti-materialist, and that the Secularism of the National Secular Society, in spite of your leadership, is crudely rationalistic and materialistic. When I called myself an atheist years ago in order to make it clear that I was on the side of Bradlaugh in his fight with the House of Commons, I meant that I had exactly the same opinion of what his persecutors called God as Mahomet had of the stones which the Arabs

worshipped before he converted them. I used a negative term to express a negative position...

When, as Nietzsche-Zarathustra put it, "God is dead", Atheism dies also. Bible-smashing is tedious to people who have smashed their Bibles. I do not say that there is no work left for atheists and Bible-smashers among people who remain steeped in the crude idolatry that is still all that religion means to large masses of the English people, though I doubt whether the line can be drawn higher now than at what the Roman Catholic Church gives up as Invincible Ignorance. But that is not my job. I prefer positive work; and, indeed, whether we like it or not, we all have to face positive work if we are to retain any hold of the pioneering section of the public. When you said, very penetratingly, in your article on my City Temple Sermon that God is in process of manufacture, you put Atheism aside just as man puts his gun aside when he has shot the tiger and must set to work with his spade. The clearing away of false solutions is not a clearing away of problems: quite the contrary: it brings you face to face with them. Denial has no further interest; you must begin to affirm.

Under this pressure there arose Neo-Darwinism, or the explanation of all phenomena as the result of Natural Selection. The world, according to this view, is only a purposeless accident, interesting only because of its amazing simulation of design and the ingenuity of its explanation. Opposed to this stands the 1790-1880 theory of Evolution as the struggle of a creative Will or Purpose (called by me the Life Force) towards higher forms of life — God in process of manufacture, as you put it. Neo-Darwinism is a materialistic theory. Evolution is a mystical one.

The Secularists embraced Natural Selection rather because it was the opposite extreme to Jehovah-worship than from any serious grasp of it and its ghastly implications. I took my own side, the mystical side, which at once brings me far nearer to Mr. Campbell, to Dr. Clifford, to the late Samuel Butler, than to any neo-Darwinian atheist. I cannot force any man to use my term Life Force to denote what he calls God; but if we both mean the same thing, and if the neo-Darwinian atheist means something profoundly different, I had better be taken to be on the theologian's side against the atheist...

Foote gave a detailed reply, vigorously disagreeing with Shaw's main points:

Atheists are not negationists because they refuse to utter shibboleths about the Unknown. They have all that really matters, all that is really positive — the Known. When I am "respectfully invited to explain the universe", I reply that I leave that job to greater and more ambitious intellects. They have been engaged on it for thousands of years, and they have not been particularly successful. When they have "land in sight", and are agreed about it, I shall be happy to listen to them.

Atheism simply means "without God", and it does not die when "God is dead". It lives and possesses the field. What dies in the final victory of Atheism is Atheistic propaganda. It is no longer needed.

Mr. Shaw does not use the word "God" yet. But I fear he is on the way to it. He believes in a conscious Life Force, a creative Will or Purpose; and he rightly judges that this places him nearer any Theist than any Atheist. At the same time, he calls it a penetrating remark of mine that "God is in process of manufacture"; the expression can only apply to a subjective reality, a conception, an ideal... (1 November, 1908.)

Shaw was, however, praised in the *Freethinker* when he opposed censorship and Blasphemy law in his privately printed "Evidence Prepared for the Censorship Committee" and his play "The Shewing Up of Blanco Posnet: a Sermon in Crude Melodrama" is approved for the main character's propensity to talk enough "blasphemy" to secure his "only begetter" twenty years' imprisonment.

Freedom of Speech

Blasphemy cases re-appeared in the twentieth century and the *Freethinker*, naturally, took a great interest. Harry Boulter was sentenced to one month's imprisonment for blasphemy while speaking at Highbury Corner in 1909. There was no weakening of opposition to Blasphemy Law, although some freethinkers had doubts about supporting cantankerous and crude speakers and a report from the N.S.S. Executive Committee printed in the *Freethinker* said, after Boulter was released from prison, "...There is no need for him to use coarse expressions or to sail too near the wind... The Freethought party, while ready to defend the right of free speech, may tire of prosecutions that could easily be avoided." Similar prosecutions were brought against Mr. Stewart and Mr. Gott in Leeds. Gott was prosecuted for selling *Rib-Ticklers*, which Foote said was "not calculated to do Freethought much good or Christianity much harm." There was an indignant condemnation of "the comic-opera crime of 'Blasphemy'. To imprison every person guilty of 'vulgar' language would be to make one half of the population maintain the other." (26 November, 1911.)

The *Freethinker* continued to see itself as a bastion of free speech. A front page article entitled "The Liberty of the Press" commented upon a round-robin in favour of the freedom of the press after an argument between the *Spectator* and the *English Review*, declaring that the liberty of the press "was won by the unsubduable courage of the 'desperate' and 'disreputable'. They might also perceive that the battle for the liberty of the press is still being carried on every week — in the *Freethinker*." (28 July, 1911.)

Petty censorship of literature was ridiculed, as when Cohen, in an article on "Saint Bowdler" described the removal of a passage uncomplimentary towards missionaries from Melville's *Typee*: "...there is one saint — Saint Bowdler — at whose shrine the Protestant country pays unceasing devotion." The *Freethinker* however, paid scant attention to the arts and could itself sound almost philistine. The notice of Oscar Wilde's death, for instance, is extremely caustic: "Oscar Wilde was not without brains, but he never had any character, in the proper sense of the word. He was a most insincere posturer, and the newspapers degrade themselves by printing a selection of his 'epigrams and paradoxes'." (9 December, 1900.)

The American moralist, Comstock, was given short shrift:

> He is an unctuous Christian. He is also secretary of the American Vice Society. He gets his living by hunting down what he calls obscenity. America has sunk so low as to let the Post Office officials confiscate any books, pamphlets, or periodicals that Anthony Comstock chooses to object to. He calls straightforward Freethought "obscenity" — indeed whatever he dislikes is "obscenity". And the American judges back up the American post office. (27 May, 1906.)

Attempts to restrain the *Freethinker* raised its anger, and the end of W.H. Smith's boycott in 1906 was greeted triumphantly. Libraries were prone to become a battle-ground for freethinkers and would-be censors, and a much publicised struggle took place in Camberwell. A Catholic on the Camberwell Council denounced the *Freethinker* for its sarcastic comments about a Christmas Eve verse in the *Daily Chronicle*; the *Freethinker* had scoffed at a reference to Mary's "bosom cream" — "That *is* fine. We have heard of mother's milk before, but mother's cream is a decided novelty." The sharpest derision was reserved for the last verse:

> Let us hail
> This virgin pale,
> Whose pure and hallowed womb
> Let Him in
> Who conquered sin
> And triumphed o'er the tomb.
>
> This is so very elegant. The physiological allusion in such exquisite taste. 'Let Him in!' Well, well! Only piety is equal to these things. (8 January, 1909.)

The Councillor's protest led to a ban from the reading room of Dulwich library, and a subsequent motion excluded the *Freethinker* from all Camberwell libraries. A *Freethinker* contributor, Arthur Moss, was a local councillor and fought the ban. A Free Speech Defence League was hurriedly formed and a public protest meeting took place at which Moss presided and a Christian councillor said he wanted fair play for the opponents of Christianity. Moss put forward a motion to the council proposing that the Bible be removed from the libraries on account of indecent passages. The motion was put, but not debated because of a ploy by which next business was moved; Moss was furious that Christians were not even prepared to defend their own book.

The First World War

As war approached, the *Freethinker* was critical of militarism and mocked the idea that Christianity could bring peace on earth. The Boy Scouts were criticised:

> Physical training everybody believes in, but there is no need whatever for this to be accompanied by a military parade that ends in providing material for an Army rather than developing useful citizens... Peace, permanent peace, will only be secured when the glamour and false greatness of militarism is killed in the minds of the people. (29 January, 1911.)

When the first Dreadnought was launched it was christened by the wife of the Archbishop of Canterbury: "Nothing we ever said in the *Freethinker* against Christianity could beat this." (22 July, 1911.) Foote feared the arms race was necessary, but regretted it: "The very fact that 'Dreadnoughts' are necessary at this time of the day is a condemnation of Christianity." (28 March, 1909.)

The attack of Christian Italy on Mohammedan Turkey provoked Foote to lecture and write on "The Crescent and the Cross". The Koran and the Bible were compared by Foote, with a challenge to the belief of the average Christian that "everything connected wtih Christianity is divine, while everything connected with Mohammedanism is devilish; and that Jesus Christ was an absolutely perfect character, while Mohammed was a low, cruel, and cunning impostor." (12 November, 1911.)

Foote continued his comparison the following week:

> Christian churches were freely allowed in Mohammedan states, at a time when no Christian state would have tolerated a Mohammedan mosque.
>
> Nor is it true that the Koran orders the massacre of women and children. Mohammed is represented as expressly saying in the Table-Talk: "Kill not the old men who cannot fight, nor young children, nor women".
>
> Sale (translator of the Koran) points out what small right the Christians have to object to the Koran in this respect. The Jews were ordered by Jehovah to kill every male in some places, and every married woman, and to keep the virgins for themselves; in other places they were to kill all, men, women, and children and leave alive nothing that breathed. Jehovah was far more cruel and bloody than Allah. And as to holy wars, why, the Christians waged such against the Mohammedans for centuries, and only ceased when they were thoroughly exhausted.
>
> There is a church of the Holy Sepulchre at Jerusalem, which is in the Sultan's dominions. Greek and Latin Christians both worship in it, and a guard of Turkish soldiers stands between them to keep them from cutting each other's throats. What a picture! And what a sarcasm on the pretensions of Christianity! (19 November, 1911.)

(Now Israeli soldiers perform the same task.)

News of the assassination of the Archduke Ferdinand provided the occasion for further musing about the value of Christianity and the Bible: "It has not yet been suggested, as far as we know, that the assassination of the Archduke Ferdinand and his wife was due to 'infidelity'. No doubt the assassins were as good Christians as the victims were. There is no need to go beyond the Bible for encouragement to assassination..." (12 July, 1914.)

The outbreak of the Great War brought horror at the tragedy of war — but most freethinkers were not pacifists. Foote wrote of the "ogre of war": "Generation after generation this frightful monster gorges himself on human flesh and blood, solacing his intervals of satiety with the wine of human tears". Nevertheless, he declared "We admit that peace at any price is as mad a policy as war at every opportunity." (16 August, 1914.)

Throughout the war the *Freethinker* opposed militarism and jingoism, and challenged the idea that War necessitated propaganda and a reduction of free speech; there was reasoned comment on conscientious objectors and support for the rights of atheists in the army.

The first Zeppelin raid brought a firm condemnation of "systematic reprisals" against the Germans. Cohen reported a meeting at which systematic reprisals were advocated and at which a vicar supported the proposal "from a Christian standpoint". Cohen reacted to the phrase with irony: "The expression is superb! It is monumental!" Perhaps with more humanity than strategy, he wrote:

> The method of raining down explosive bombs on sleeping towns and cities which have not the slightest sign of fortifications is villainous enough in all conscience. And its stupidity is equal to its villainy. For if the Zeppelins managed to do ten times the damage they inflict, and murder ten times as many civilians, it could have no appreciable effect on the course of the War, save to stiffen our backs and make everybody more resolved than ever to see the thing through. Nor am I quite convinced that if our airmen kill German women and children, it will make their airmen less assiduous in attempting to kill ours. It is a common observation that brutality brutalises he that gives as much, or even more, than he who receives... (24 October, 1915.)

The *Freethinker* never succumbed to the prejudice that all Germans and German culture were barbaric. Cohen often observed, with amusement, the contradiction by which the national press saw the Germans as both a Christian and an uncivilised nation. John Smith, who wrote numerous articles for the *Freethinker* under the pseudonym of "Mimnermus", in an article entitled "Bayonets and Beatitudes" lamented that "The countrymen of Molière are cutting the throats of the countrymen of Goethe, and the compatriots of Kossuth are disembowelling the brothers of Tolstoy... Think of it! Whole nations, professedly Christian, engaged in wholesale murder." (23 August, 1914.) And Cohen roundly challenged jingoistic philistinism: "The value of Goethe's philosophy and poetry, of Wagner's, or Beethoven's, or Schubert's music, the work of German scientists, is not in the smallest degree affected by the barbarities of Germans in Belgium and France, or by the inflated military ambitions of the Kaiser and his supporters." (20 September, 1914.)

As the war progressed the Churches spoke of a Christian revival and organised days of intercession for peace; there were also evangelical campaigns. Horatio Bottomley, editor of *John Bull*, was taken to task for changing his views to suit the national mood. An article "John Bull and God" wondered why Mr. Bottomley, whom the *Freethinker* had always considered an agnostic, offered "a dose of pietistic jingoism." The words of Mr. Bottomley quoted in the *Freethinker* indicate, by contrast, how restrained and reasonable was the tone of the *Freethinker* during the war: " 'God moves in a mysterious way his wonders to perform' and the wonder he is now performing is the riddance of Europe, and mankind, of the Teutonic menace to His Scheme of Things." (20 September, 1914.)

The *Freethinker* suggested that the alleged increase in religion due to the war was exaggerated, and quoted the Christian, Dr. Campbell Morgan, who "fears there is a certain amount of unbelief arising as a result of the War. Many, he says, give way to a 'fierce resentful agnosticism'." (25 April, 1915.) A letter from "A Soldier Atheist" recorded that there was little use for Christianity in the Trenches:

> ...Parsons and others have claimed that the War and its hardships have brought out the religion of the soldier. I give it the direct lie. I know that in actual fact the soldier, when at his task in this bloodiest of wars, has no time for God and religion. A clean rifle, well-fitting bayonet, keen eye, and steady nerve — these are necessary assets. The German gives us no time for psalm-singing, and we in our turn ask for none and give none.
>
> ...But there live in peace, away behind the firing-line, the Army Chaplains. They are all sleek, comfortable, well paid, and well clothed. Sunday comes, and with it a compulsory Church Service. The men hate it — loathe it. (14 November, 1915.)

Conscientious Objectors

The *Freethinker* reported exchanges from the tribunal examining conscientious objectors; there was especial interest in the way Christian and atheist arguments were considered. An Acid Drop reported an exemption tribunal where "One Christian objects to service as the Bible says 'Thou shalt not kill', and straightway some member of the tribunal quotes 'I come not to bring peace but a sword'. Others have based their objections to the teaching that Jesus suffered aggression uncomplainingly, and have been promptly assured that one mustn't imitate him in that nowadays." (12 March, 1916.) Later a correspondent reported a tribunal that asked a freethinker if he believed in God, and when he said " 'No, not with this awful slaughter' was told 'Then you have not got a conscience. We do not admit your claim.' " (16 April, 1916.)

A long letter from Bertrand Russell to the *Freethinker* discussed the position of conscientious objectors. Russell complained that objectors were sometimes not given absolute exemption, but forced into work which they felt supported the war effort. He also stressed that unbelievers can be men of conscience:

> Almost all the Tribunals have taken the view that a man cannot have a conscientious objection to war unless he belongs to a religious body which has this for one of its explicit principles. But conscience is an individual thing, and forbids to one man what it allows to another. Many who are conscientious objectors are filled with an intense desire to serve the community, but they believe (strange as this belief must appear to those who do not share it) that they can best serve the community by trying to turn men against the war...

Russell wrote that it was natural that those whose sons or brothers are in the trenches should think they are "escaping more lightly than the young men who are fighting for their country" but commented:

> I am not sure that this is true. The moral suffering in standing out against public opinion, often against parents and friends, and in incurring obloquy and the taunt of cowardice, is not an easy thing to bear. The instinct of sacrifice is strong in many of those who refuse to fight, and it has been almost unbearable to them that their belief forbade them to share the hardships and dangers of the battlefield. They are glad that the time has come when they, too, must suffer for their cause.
>
> But how will the nation gain by making them suffer?...
>
> These men believe, rightly or wrongly, that the evils of militarism and the atrocities that the war has brought forth will never be extirpated by fighting. They believe that militarism can only be destroyed by pacifism, and that hate can only be killed by love. There were such men in Germany. It has been reported that many have been shot in that country. But no punishment can prove them mistaken; punishment can only prove their sincerity in the eyes of the doubting public. They believe that, with faith and courage, passive resistance is more unconquerable than bayonets; and if the authorities choose to put them to the test, they are prepared to demonstrate the truth of their own belief by their own endurance. (14 May, 1916.)

Cohen did not agree and had earlier written of a manifesto of the Society of Friends on war resistance:

> Unqualified non-resistance is a sheer absurdity. Qualified resistance only means in effect not resisting more than is necessary. In practice it means the substitution of one form of resistance for another. It was possible for the Society of Friends, individually or collectively, to disclaim the use of force, because they were living in a society which applied the measure of force necessary for their protection. (23 August, 1914.)

Later Cohen wrote that it was illogical of the Government to propose compulsory conscription and then allow exemptions; without actually opposing it, he regretted that the introduction of the Military Service Bill "marks one more step along the road of social demoralization which, as was pointed out last week, invariably accompanies war." "Militarism" or "Prussianism" was condemned because "It establishes the soldier, not as a hateful, a deplorable necessity, but as an indispensable part of our normal life." (16 January, 1916.)

War Propaganda

An aspect of the demoralisation of the War which the *Freethinker* especially opposed was the propaganda and attempts at reducing free speech. At first it was feared that reference to the War on public platforms was to be completely forbidden (30 August, 1914), but Foote lectured on "Religion, War and Humanity". Cohen disapproved of any suppression of public debate: "... is it a good thing that political and social disputes should cease and the community satisfy itself with the uniform monotony of a hive of bees?" (25 October, 1914.) When clerics reported a reduction in internal strife as a benefit of the war, Cohen wrote: "Party politics and social conflicts and feminist agitation were at least disputes about the better ordering of social life. It is along that road — the path of discussion, agitation, and experiment — that progress lies." (2 January, 1916.)

Cohen wrote about the "intensive war-propaganda" ("Thanks to the Northcliffe influence") in his recollections of the *Freethinker's* past in the "Jubilee Supplement":

> Just at the beginning of 1916 I received a visit from two men who professed to be Freethinkers and business men in the City. I did not know them, nor could I find out, from their conversation, any Freethinker who did. But they professed a great interest in the paper, and thought that the time had arrived when it might be turned into a company, and they were willing to purchase. I listened to what they had to say, and was doubtful whether I had to compliment them upon their business philanthropy or sympathise with their financial folly. I found afterwards that one at least of the two was a government agent. He came into notice through inciting a Derbyshire school teacher to concoct a fantastic plan to poison Lloyd George, and then acted as an informer. (10 May, 1931.)

Others approached him to induce him to preach war.

> My reply to these was that there were plenty to preach war, without my adding my voice to the number. Besides, I would take no hand in disseminating the fantastic tales that were abroad, or to make more difficult the solution of peace problems once the war came to an end. It was not the business of the *Freethinker* to oppose war, and it was certainly not its business to join in the foolish talk of seventy millions of people being made up of none but scoundrels and degenerates. We were at war, and more than ever was it necessary to do what one could to keep men's heads level, and to see that feelings of common decency and justice were not completely forgotten. Moreover, *Freethinker* readers had not been accustomed to finding in the paper only that with which they were in agreement. The *Freethinker* might die, but if it died it would go down with its flag flying, true to both its name and its policy. (Ibid.)

Conflict with the authorities came when Cohen wrote about the Russian steam-rollers and pointed out that "the tales about the wild enthusiasm for the war could not be depended upon." He received a suggestion that he submit such paragraphs for censorship. "I replied curtly that there never had been a censor in the *Freethinker* office, and so far as I was concerned I had no intention of setting one up." On another occasion when two men in military uniform requested to see the *Freethinker*'s subscribers list, Cohen refused and when he was asked if he took any care to see that the paper did not get into enemy hands retorted "Not the slightest." "I said if the Emperor of Germany sent along twopence half-penny for the *Freethinker,* it would be posted to the address given."

Other issues of censorship during the war years included vigorous opposition to the London County Council's attempt to ban the sale of literature in public parks, and the continuing matter of blasphemy, though all attempts to abolish Blasphemy Law were now shelved. An attempt by Lord Alfred Douglas, living out a religiose later life, to bring about a blasphemy prosecution against George Moore's fictional account of the life of Jesus, *The Book of Kerith*, failed, and the *Freethinker* noted with optimism that despite the book's "frank disregard for the supernatural" it had been received without outrage.

Determination "to keep the flag flying" in opposition to censorship and to sustain a voice of reason at a time of war, when many journals vanished, upheld the *Freethinker* during the war years. A severe problem was the increase in cost and shortage of paper — a difficulty to which Cohen made continual reference: "The Government had placed fortunes within the reach of paper merchants, and they were not slow to avail themselves of the opportunity." But the deepest impact of the Great War upon freethinkers was the jolt it gave to what had sometimes been an over-easy belief in progress. This was faced with honesty by Cohen writing in a New Year column on "The Outlook":

> That there should be a war at all, of the kind that exists, is enough to make one incline to pessimism over the future of European nations. For years many of us have gone on preaching the superiority of reason over brute force; extolling the advances of science and the progress of civilisation, until we had got into the habit of feeling rather than thinking, that war between the leading civilised nations of Europe was an impossibility... We are forcibly reminded that after all we may have overestimated the solidity of our civilisation. (3 January, 1915.)

Secular Society Ltd. in the Courts

Among the achievements of which Foote was most proud was the foundation of Secular Society Ltd. The *Freethinker* had never been financially secure — and the editor sacrificed his personal financial security for the sake of the cause[1]). (He does not seem to have been financially astute!) Numerous appeals testify both to the generosity of *Freethinker* readers of humble circumstances and the lack of funds which the journal continuously faced. An injustice and penalty to freethought organisations was the prevention of bequests, because legacies to any society with illegal objects, such as blasphemy, could be declared null and void. This had happened with £500 left to a Secular Hall scheme in 1885, where courts had upheld the executors' refusal to hand over the money. While reflecting upon Lord Coleridge's judgment that "if the decencies of controversy are observed, even the fundamentals of religion may be attacked without a person being guilty of blasphemous libel", Foote devised a method for legally securing funds from bequests for secular purposes. He thought that the creation of a separate limited

1)There is evidence of financial irresponsibility such as borrowing from all and sundry without being punctilious about returning loans. See an unpublished memoir of C.A. Watts in the possession of the Rationalist Press Association.

company would solve the difficulty and was prepared to test it in the courts. After much thought and legal advice a form of Memorandum and Articles of a Company Limited by Guarantee, with the advantages of a Trust but with the rights of individual citizens, was worked out; and Secular Society Ltd was founded in 1898.

Many bequests were received and Secular Society Ltd was important in putting secularism upon a firmer financial footing. Mr. C. Bowman bequeathed his possessions to Secular Society Ltd in 1908, but left them in trust for his widow. On her death in 1914 the legacy became due to be received by Secular Society Ltd, but the Trustees, acting on behalf of a relative, challenged the bequest on the grounds that "the Society is unlawful and against public welfare." In April 1915 a case was brought before Mr. Justice Joyce, who upheld the legality of the Society and hence the bequest. An Appeal in July was dismissed. An article in the *Freethinker* praised Foote, whose inspiration the whole business had been, for a "magnificent victory". The case established that it is not illegal to deny the truth of religion, and also had significant implications in the wider field of trust law.

After a further appeal, the House of Lords in May 1917 again upheld the legality of the bequest to Secular Society Ltd. A front page headline in the *Freethinker* read "A Secular Charter" and began triumphantly: "History was made in the House of Lords on Monday, May 14. For more than two years the Secular Society, Limited, has been fighting in one court after another, ostensibly to secure a legacy properly bequeathed it, really to establish a principle that will carry us another step along the road of mental emancipation." The significance to the *Freethinker* was the point, which was admitted by a comment on the case in the *Church Times*: "England is no longer in law, as it has ceased to be in fact, a Christian country."

Cohen wrote that the decision should be seen as a starting point for further reform:

> The outcome of the House of Lords' judgment should be, then, the creation of a more insistent attempt to disestablish religion and to wipe out the Blasphemy Laws altogether. So long as these latter remain on the statute books they are a constant menace to real freedom... And the Freethought Party will fall short of its duty if it does not utilize this magnificent victory as a stepping-stone to still greater triumphs. (3 June, 1917.)

Death of Foote

A major event in the history of the *Freethinker* occurred in October 1915, when G.W. Foote, editor since 1881, died. His health had been failing for some while and many a "Personal Note" in the *Freethinker* referred to his health difficulties. Chapman Cohen was already playing a key role editing the *Freethinker* before Foote's death and was the natural heir apparent. In his last months, though Foote continued to write for the

Freethinker, he was often too ill to walk and enjoyed being taken in a bath-chair along the cliffs near his home in Westcliffe-on-Sea.

His domestic life had been contented to the end. According to Mimnermus "The family dispensed a cordial hospitality, the house being seldom without visitors and friends." (G.W. Foote. — As A Man. 7 November, 1915.) Among his most prized possessions were a portrait of Colonel Ingersoll with an inscription in Ingersoll's handwriting, a portrait of Richard Carlile, and an inscribed volume of Meredith's poems sent to him while he was in prison.

He was known for his kindness and good-humour. Once, when he gave a sovereign to "a poor derelict", Mimnermus said he feared it would be spent in a public house: "He flashed his eyes on me, and said, 'What of it? He will be happy for an hour or so!' " Two aspects of his temperament were commented upon by many who wrote about him in the *Freethinker* after his death: his ready wit and his powerful speaking ability. "Once when he had been lecturing on 'An Hour in Hell', a clergyman present complained of his cruel attack on religious belief. 'I am not cruel,' replied Mr. Foote. 'If I took the audience to hell, I brought them back again.' " Mimnermus also described his powers of public speaking: "All who knew him must remember his beautiful, soft voice, with its marvellous range. Always individual, he invested his recitals with his own personality. His rendering of Hood's *Bridge of Sighs* and of Tennyson's *Rizpah* were revelations."

Tributes came from far and wide and many freethinkers attended his funeral at the City of London crematorium. Cohen said in an address that "Freethought in this country has been so long identified with George William Foote that it was almost inconceivable without him." And William Heaford, a *Freethinker* contributor and friend of Foote, wrote with affection and admiration:

> We who knew and loved G.W. Foote and admired the brilliancy of his genius are perhaps too near the object of our regard to be able to view him in due perspective in relation to the ulterior trend and tendency of the stirring heroic times out of which he grew, and of which he became the latest and sublime embodiment and representative. The wider catholicity of spirit which Mr. Foote's life-work certainly made possible for friend and foe alike may, for aught we know, transform our methods and uplift our ideals. In any case, whether we continue fighting in the old trenches, with the old shot and shrapnel and asphyxiating gasses assailing us, or are able to take the battle forward to a new stage made possible by the ground freshly won for us by the heroic services of our dead Chief, the name of G.W. Foote will always be cherished in the grateful veneration of countless generations of Freethinkers. Though dead, his example and inspiration will ever speak to our hearts and stir within us, and in those to whom we hand forward the good old tradition, an abiding love of the good old cause. (31 October, 1915.)

And it shall come to pass that I will put thee in a clift of the rock, and I shall take away my hand, and thou shalt see my back parts.—EXODUS xxxiii., 23.

DIVINE ILLUMINATION.

"And God said, Let there be light: and there was light."—
Genesis i., 3.

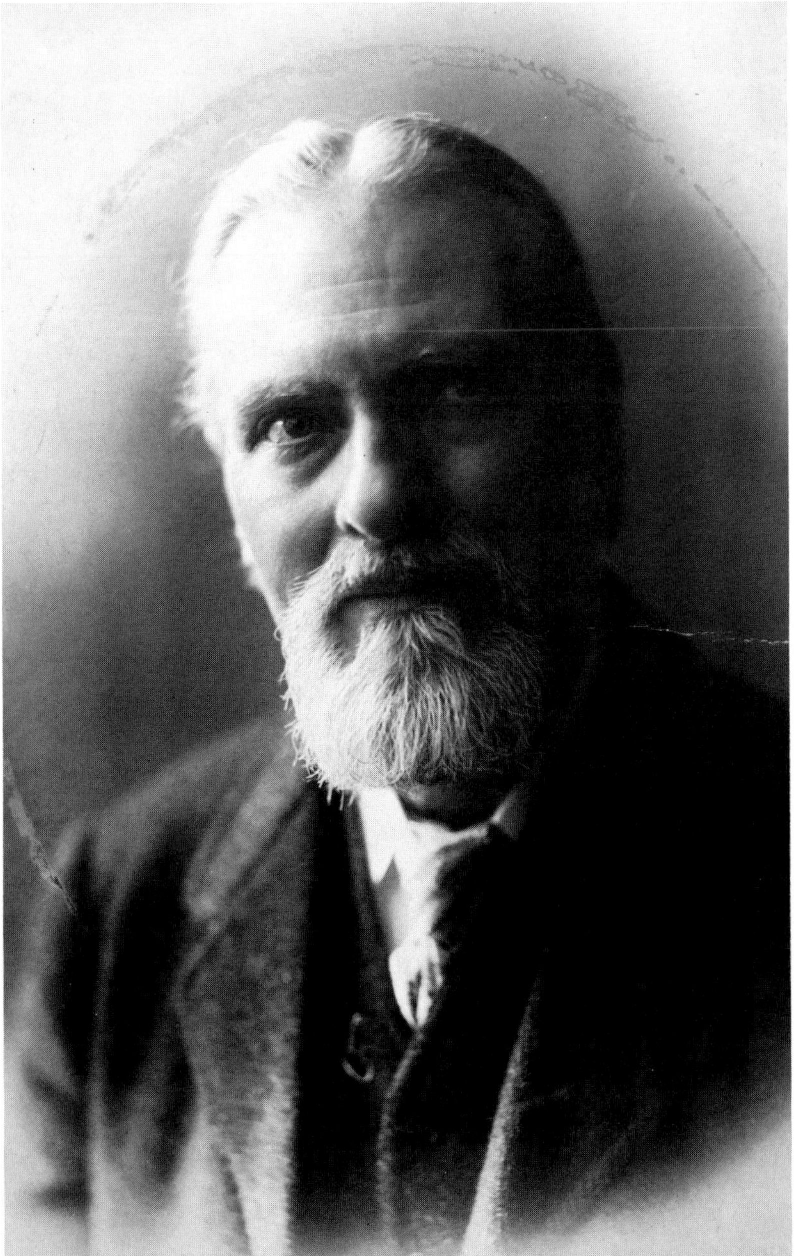

George William Foote.

Chapman Cohen.

Three Editors cut the cake at the Centenary Celebrations:
William McIlroy, Jim Herrick, Kit Mouat (L to R)

Photo. by Barry Duke.

CHAPTER IV
THE INTER-WAR YEARS: COMBATING AUTHORITARIANISM

During the war years the death of Foote and the legal case against Secular Society Ltd were events of lasting significance to the *Freethinker;* Cohen was established firmly in the helm for nearly 40 years and without financial stability survival would have been impossible. The shattering of belief in progress and confident optimism was a momentous legacy of the war to twentieth century freethought.

The conclusion of the Great War brought a predictable response from the *Freethinker,* which castigated those who, like Lloyd George, asked the nation to thank God for the peace:

> Are we to thank God for the twenty millions of deaths the war has cost the world? Or for the fact that we have had four years of one of the most brutal wars in history?... Really, the less said about God the better. God does nothing. That is certainly one of the lessons of the War. (17 November, 1918.)

Scepticism towards a belief that could fit so terrible a war into a divine pattern rippled beyond the circle of avowed freethinkers. Somerset Maugham's play *The Unknown* produced in 1920 contained a mother who had lost two sons in the war and asked "Who is going to forgive God?" Maugham said in an interview about the play that "no one can fail to see that the ideas we have been brought up on about the loving mercy of God are rather shattered." The *Mirror* headed an article "Did the War Kill Men's Faith?" and the *Freethinker* said "Mr. Maugham's play is concerned with the exposure of two lies — the lie of militarism and the lie of religion." (22 August, 1920.)

The Kaiser, who was excessively militarist and religious, was an embarrassment to the pious and the *Freethinker* pointed this out:

> The ex-Kaiser used to figure among the subscribers to the British Foreign and Bible Society, and only since the War has his name been deleted from the annual reports. His piety was so pronounced that on one occasion he actually forbade the erection of a statue to Heine on the grounds of the poet's infidelity. As a fact, no one doubted Wilhelm's religiosity until Christians found it convenient to drop him. (22 December, 1918.)

The *Freethinker* joined with those who saw the end of the war as a time for new possibilities: "The War of armed force is ended; the war of ideas is about to begin." (24 November, 1918.) Even before the end of the war the *Freethinker* had looked to the future and suggested that when the "Khaki army" was demobilised, the "Black army" of priests might also be disbanded and put to "some form of social employment and recognized utility and service. They could help to teach people how to live, instead of explaining to them how to die. They would teach people to rely upon their own intelligence and strength instead of upon the expected help of an antiquated tribal fetish." (27 January, 1918.)

Cohen was quick to see the dangers of creating a peace that could not endure: "if some of our leaders have their way, the Peace will contain the seeds of future wars..." — a prescient observation. The *Freethinker* was enthusiastic about the idea of the League of Nations, pointing out that it had been a dream of Thomas Paine more than a century previously. However, the *Freethinker* was consistent for twenty years in criticising the likely ineffectiveness of an organisation which was composed of nation states all unwilling to sacrifice any of their power.

> But it is idle to dream of a Peace of Nations while this or that nation maintains an Army or Navy strong enough to wage war either on its own account or in combination with others. This is a return to the old system of alliances,defensive and offensive. A real League of Nations means giving as well as taking. It means surrendering the power to attack in return for security from aggression. (5 January, 1919.)

When the Peace between Germany and the Allies was signed a front page of the *Freethinker* stressed the importance of the League of Nations "because peace is everyone's business," but the emphasis on nationalism was thought wrong, the title "League of Peoples" being preferred: " 'Nation' still carries with it a notion of separateness, of a defensive attitude of mind that is an invitation to attack, of the 'My country right or wrong' attitude that was so powerful a factor in Germany perpetuating the War... Nationalism is at best an evolutionary phase of the journey to internationalism, just as tribalism was a stage on the journey to nationalism." (25 January, 1920.) Cohen wrote, regretfully, in 1936:

> There is very little satisfaction in being able to say "I told you so", but the pitiful collapse of the League of Nations forces us to say it. Ever since 1919 we have stressed the point that the League was bound to fail so long as it was constituted by the old governmental gangs, each of which was trying to steal a march on the others, not one of them ready to trust the others, and continuing the policy of saying one thing in public and another in private. (10 May, 1936.)

The post-war mood was, in Cohen's opinion, a factor in the increased popularity of spiritualism. An article on "The Shady Side of Spiritualism" commented on Conan Doyle's shift from Sherlock Holmes to "Mr. Sludge the Medium": "The present recrudescence of Spiritualism is largely caused by the heavy death-toll of the great war. There is a quite natural desire among the bereaved to seek for consolation through almost any channel... The money the 'medium' rakes in is the flow of tears from the sorrowful and distressed, and is one of the shadiest of shady businesses." (23 March, 1919.) Cohen, writing on "The Spiritualistic Boom", emphasised that "after the prolonged strain of a huge war, everyone's nerves have been at a tension, the emotional strain has been great, and nothing so multiplies the chances of delusion and illusion as that..." (20 July, 1919.)

An article, signed E.J.D., which castigated Conan Doyle for believing unreliable witnesses, produced a sharp retort from the prolific writer turned spiritualist propagandist:

> I see that your contributor, E.J.D., accounts for the remarkable phenomenon examined in the case of Mr. Slade by Zollner and his friends by the assertion that Zollner was ill, that Fechner was blind, and that Weber and Scheibner were imbeciles. I have not yet found out what form of paresis I am myself suffering from, but as our opponents invariably affix some bodily affliction upon everyone who believes the evidence in favour of psychic force, I have only to await my turn. (8 February, 1920.)

The post-war period saw gropings for changes in society — with discussion of the position of women, with socialism, with greater freedom to talk about human sexuality, with the growth of the film industry and beginnings of a national broadcasting system. The *Freethinker* took an interest in such changes, although the format and content of many of the articles about the Bible and religion retained a feel of the nineteenth century.

Feminist Issues

Before the War was over the franchise was extended to most women over thirty in a Representation of the People Bill which was passed in the House of Lords in December 1917. The Bishops voted for it, though without enthusiasm. The Archbishop of Canterbury described the extension of the franchise as "a leap in the dark", but acknowledged "there was a great change of public opinion" and warned of the consequences of bishops placing themselves in opposition to public opinion.

Cohen's comment that "they voted for what it was not safe to oppose" is apt for much of the bishops' reluctant acquiescence to social change in has no ideas to get saved by, he has none worth being damned for, and he will always give way if the pressure be strong enough." Cohen was caustic about "the historic teaching and practice of the Christian Churches in relation to women. No other institution has so uniformly and so universally denied to women legal equality as the Christian Church has done, and no institution was so powerful in moulding public sentiment in this direction." (20 January, 1918.)

Although the *Freethinker* has not been prominent in campaigning for women's suffrage, the rights of women were always seen as part of the radical freethought tradition. "The triumph of the Women's Suffrage Movement is a victory for Freethought, and the belated recognition of the rights of women is a tribute to the pioneers from Mary Wollstonecraft to John Stuart Mill." (27 January, 1918.) Cohen foresaw women as malleable election material for church interests and noted that the Catholic Women's League had responded to the new franchise by stating that "Catholic women must be educated to do their duty well..." Cohen commented "In other words, when the clergy pull the strings the marionettes will vote." (10 February, 1918.)

In a rather rare note of enthusiasm for feminism, as opposed to disaffection with the Christian attitude to women, Cohen wrote, in an article on "Women and Christianity":

> Woman is awakening at last. One half the human race is in revolt against the dominance of the other half. And it is important to note that a very large proportion of those in revolt are not blind to the existence of the real enemy. [The churches.] (9 November, 1919.)

When complete equality of franchise was given to women in 1928, it was welcomed by Cohen: "Personally, I think it is a reform that is long overdue, and it has always been one of the immediate objects of the National Secular Society to secure the equality of the sexes before the law — subject to such differences as nature has imposed." (1 April, 1928.) His reaction to the question then being asked in the *Evening Standard*, "Should the Church Admit Women Priests?" was less enthusiastic: "I do not think so meanly of the intelligence of women as to think they will rush to fill a profession that is lower today than at any time in the history of modern Europe." (Ibid.)

The Churches were also reluctant to countenance the idea of laws making divorce more straightforward. An unsuccessful attempt at Divorce Law reform in 1920 was noticed in the *Freethinker*: "The Assistant Postmaster-General informed the House as to the "teaching of Christ' on the subject, and the members never laughed at the absurdity of settling the matter of divorce in 1920 by an appeal to what a celibate Jewish teacher of 2,000 years ago is reported to have said on the subject." (25 April, 1920.)

The letter columns, which became a more vigorous forum of debate during this period, had earlier contained a plea for reform from M.L. Seaton-Siedeman, the Secretary of the Divorce Law Reform Union:

> Every measure for the true welfare of the community has been opposed by the Churches. We are only asking for a remedy for a cancer that exists in our national life. We want cleaner marriages, fewer or no irregular unions, and a legitimate birth-rate, instead of opposing a reform of the present iniquitous divorce law, and advocating the perpetuation of a system which is responsible for a vast amount of avoidable misery and crime, the Churches would, indeed, do well if they could forthwith undertake to educate the young children and adolescents that come under their influence into the true meaning of marriage, in its physical, mental, and spiritual aspects, then we shall have reason to hope that the higher ideal of marriage, about which we are as keen as they, will be realized.
>
> Ours is the remedy; theirs the opportunity. (16 June, 1918.)

The Roman Catholic Church, the increasing power of which was a matter of continuous comment in the twenties and thirties, was seen as a prime enemy of rational marital relationships:

> The Pope has issued an encyclical on the question of marriage, divorce, and birth control. He will have nothing to do with birth control, and his decision is, of course, binding on all Roman Catholics. He does not care what kind of children are born so long as they are born in sufficient numbers to give the Church a crop sufficiently large to keep the Roman Church, numerically, on top. He does not care how unhappy or disastrous marriages are — unless they are contracted by people in high position

> whom it will profit the church to accommodate — and there can be no divorce. (18 January, 1931.)

The *Freethinker,* always sympathetic to the view that women should be given the ability to control their own fertility, allowed oblique discussion of the neo-Malthusian question to give way to direct debate about birth control. Dora Russell's opinions from the *Lansbury's Labour Weekly* were quoted with approval:

> Personally, I do not believe that traditional religious teaching has anything to contribute to solving human problems. Its view of human nature itself is superficial and unsound. It has failed in the past and is still failing. Birth control, to me as to others, comes in as part of a very different view of life, which is as important to us as Roman Catholicism to devout believers. (27 September, 1925.)

Among women freethinkers the matter could be controversial and Frances Prewett wrote:

> Freethinkers are doing the worst possible disservice to their cause by associating it with such a temporary masculine expedient as Neo-Malthusian practices. No modern organisation can hope to advance if it lack the support of earnest, intelligent women; but if Freethought be indissolubly coupled with degrading the supreme function of womanhood to the uses of sense, then the fine spiritual woman will stand aside from the Freethought movement. (3 October, 1920.)

This untypical view was challenged in a letter from a woman demonstrating the more positive attitude to human sexuality that was gaining currency:

> Any woman of normal sexual development possesses sexual passion in much the same proportion as a normally developed man, and this quite apart from any maternal instinct — which instinct is enormously exaggerated! It is still more absurd for a modern woman of freethinking principles to deprecate sexual indulgence (as if she were a bishop hurling forth denunciation!), when it is the natural outcome of a perfectly natural and healthy instinct. (10 October, 1920.)

Marie Stopes was applauded by the *Freethinker* for publicly condemning the "insolent" attitude of "unmarried Bishops" on the subject of birth control — "Their unnatural and unhealthy attitude towards sex should be swept away." But there were doubts about "her other utterance that she was out to smash the tradition of organized Christianity and to enthrone Christ's own tradition of wholesome, healthy love towards sex life." The *Freethinker* suggested she would be "well-advised to attempt no compromise with the religion which has always degraded her sex..." (12 April, 1925.)

Such advice was unlikely to be followed by Marie Stopes, for she had earlier repudiated any association between herself and atheists. In a letter to the *Northern Echo,* she wrote:

> I should be much obliged if you will give me this opportunity of making public the very essential difference between my message and that of Bradlaugh and Besant. They were fundamentally Freethinkers and Atheists... My message, on the other hand, is in the name of God, and is

> delivered essentially as an extension of Christ's own teaching, specially applicable to the needs of the present community and rendered possible by recent advances in knowledge.

Quoting her letter in a front page article on "Religion and 'Birth Control' ", Cohen reproved Dr. Stopes for rejecting her debt to Bradlaugh and Besant:

> No recognition of the truth that without this fight (of Bradlaugh and Besant), in all probability, Dr. Stopes' Mothers' Clinic would never have existed, for in the face of her letter one can hardly picture her doing what Bradlaugh and Besant did; no word of thanks for Bradlaugh having started the Malthusian League nearly sixty years ago, nor of the important circumstance that Bradlaugh went into the fight for the express purpose of establishing the right to publicly discuss the very thing for which Dr. Stopes now claims public sympathy and support. (17 April, 1921.)

A general complaint about the tendency to underestimate freethought contributions to social reform followed:

> If one takes the reforms of the last century only, reforms in the world of labour, of education, in criminology, in the enfranchisement of women, and in the establishment of free speech and of free publication, it is the work of the despised Freethinker which stands out most clearly, not that of those who spoke "in the name of God". Yet as the reformers gain ground it is always the common, the religious type of mind, that steps in and reaps the credit for what has been accomplished". (Ibid.)

An extreme view on birth control came in an article by A.F. Williams on "Annihilation — or Sterilization?" The dangers of population expansion remain relevant, but the ideas about perfection of the human race contain an unpleasant totalitarian ring:

> Future wars will be caused by children. Wars for religion or revenge are things of the past; reason and bitter experience tell us of their futility. Too many children and too little room or food will FORCE nations to war, slowly but inevitably, although perhaps they would cavil at bloodshed for "honour" or a "scrap of Paper". Expansion is the new cause of conflict..
>
> Sterilization must come. Voluntary in economic stress or compulsory in disease-ridden or insane partners, it will be the accepted dogma of the next decade. Birth-control, once the greatest heresy and "evil" is here, and here to stay. There will be sufficient children born whatever restriction schemes come into being, for people WILL have them. Quality and not quantity will perfect the race: restriction (obviously of the possibly unfit and unemployable at first) and not fostering, of child-birth is what is wanted. (19 April, 1936.)

(The *Agnostic Journal* moved further in this direction than the *Freethinker* ever did.).

A letter on birth control in 1931 also discussed abortion, which, although opposed, was at least being referred to in a reasonable way: "The problem of abortion will turn ultimately on a sentiment. The question of destroying a new-born child may need 'calm and careful consideration', but this will be, in the last resort, the calm and careful consideration of basic feelings." (4 January, 1931.)

During a trial for two cases of abortion, later in the same year, Mr. Justice McCardie said that the law with regard to abortion was sadly out of date and a knowledge of birth control ought to be widely circulated among the working classes. The *Church Times* regretted that a judge should oppose accepted Christian concepts and Cohen reflected upon the inevitable clash between religion and a sane judicature, adding the usual rider about "the unhealthy Christian attitude to sex — Christianity did not make sex passion pure, it only made it furtive." (13 December, 1931.)

Sexuality and Free Speech

The *Freethinker* endorsed a freer and more scientific attitude to sexuality. Havelock Ellis's *Psychology of Sex* was quoted in an article "Fettered Thought in Sex Problems" by C.M.B. The sex instinct was seen as quite natural: "Enough evil already exists from repression of the normal sex instinct. Hysteria, religious mania, and other neuroses are, in the majority of cases, but the outward and visible sign of mate hunger; prudery is almost invariably but camouflaged desire." (10 October, 1920.)

Chapman Cohen often expanded on his view that sexual and religious feelings were connected, and covered the question fully in *Religion and Sex*, one of the few of his books not based mainly on previously written articles.

Sex education was supported and a Sugar Plum item expressed pleasure at "a letter in the *Leeds Mercury*, signed 'Infidel', pleading for greater candour towards the young with regard to sex knowledge. We feel it is the safer and wiser way." (15 February, 1920.) An article on "Christianity and Sex" recommended Etie Rout's *Sexual Health and Birth Control* to all freethinkers, and affirmed that "It is Christianity which is responsible for the idea that there is something essentially horrid and sinful about sex." There was a suggestion that the pious preferred ignorance, being afraid that "if the knowledge of how to prevent venereal disease became known, it would enable men to be immoral without suffering for it." (22 March, 1925.)

A fictional dialogue, which must have seemed very advanced to some readers, showed an Army Medical Officer and an Army Chaplain arguing about VD — an argument in which prevention and hygiene won an overwhelming victory over retribution and abstinence.

The generally freer attitude to sexual matters was seen in an enthusiastic piece by 'Mimnermus' about Walt Whitman on the centenary of his birth: "Take his attitude towards sex and the body. For the lover there is nothing in the beloved impure and unclean. This conception of purity is but a poetic rendering of the purity and beauty of organic life. It is a lesson sorely needed in our over-strained civilization." (18 August, 1918.) However, the article contains no reference to Whitman's homosexuality or the homoerotic content of some of his poems. There were in the *Freethinker* references to Havelock Ellis, who was a pioneer student of what he called "sexual inversion", and protest that his work on the physiology and psychology of sex was not available — "for directly it was published it was pounced on by these mentally diseased carrion crows, prosecuted for indecency and ordered to be destroyed." (2 September, 1928.) The prosecution of the novel about lesbians, *The Well of Loneliness* by Radclyffe Hall, in 1928, brought the first direct reference to homosexuality in the *Freethinker.*

The Well of Loneliness was a book which, according to the *Freethinker* "deals with the problem of 'masculine woman' — the woman endowed with the mentality of a man..." (2 September, 1928.) It was attacked by the editor of the *Sunday Express,* James Douglas — "a Christian editor", and a *bête noir* of the *Freethinker.* The publisher, Jonathan Cape, "in a panic, sent the book to the Home Office to avoid the prosecution he evidently feared would follow this ignorant tirade." The Home Secretary, Sir William Joynson-Hicks, was a notorious prude and "moral crusader" and he predictably declared *The Well of Loneliness* unfit for circulation. Cape withdrew the book and was accused in the *Freethinker,* by W. Mann in an article called "The New 'Index Expurgatorious' ", of "letting us down". The book was said by E.M. Forster and Virginia Woolf, in a letter to *The Nation,* to be "restrained and perfectly decent, and the treatment of its theme unexceptionable." (Quoted, 16 September, 1928.) A prosecution should have been fought in defence of free speech, according to the *Freethinker.*

Another edition of *The Well of Loneliness* was printed in Paris and copies sent to England were confiscated by the Custom House Officials. At the magistrates court the book was condemned because "the writer introduced the name of the Deity into the book to support her plea" and because "she did not hold up certain forms of abnormal sexual conduct to 'condemnation'." Chapman Cohen wrote, in a comment which moves tentatively towards gay rights:

> The reference to the Deity is that the authoress makes one of her characters say they are made by God, and they demand fair treatment and proper recognition. Well, if there is no God, the language is idle. If there is a God, then these people are God's handiwork, and have a right to demand consideration at the hands of their creator. The other point is that the writer asked that these people should be treated with toleration and sympathy. Why not? Science does not condemn, it teaches us to understand, and enlightened understanding brings toleration and sympathy. The overwhelming mass of cultured opinion would be in favour of extending sympathy to people who were cursed in the way these people are cursed. Condemnation is quite out of place. One might as reasonably condemn a man for being born with some inherited disease. (25 November, 1928.)

The appeal against the magistrates' order for the seized copies to be destroyed failed. Eminent writers, who defended the book, included Rudyard Kipling, Julian Huxley, Shaw, H.G. Wells and Arnold Bennett. The *Freethinker* said: "Can anyone in their senses believe that all the greatest writers of our time have banded together to praise a book if it is really 'disgusting' and 'obscene' as these magistrates declare?" (30 December, 1928.)

The *Freethinker* sustained its defence of free speech for "advanced" literature, which cannot have appealed to many of its readers, and for political views for which Cohen had no sympathy. A comparison between the twenties and the "Roaring Yellow Nineties" declared "Our emancipation nowadays is amazing... Our daughters use their German to read the plays of Wedekind, and their French to study the charming confessions of sexual abnormalities collected for us by Mr. Havelock Ellis in his *Études de psychologie sexuelle*" (31 October, 1920.)

When two British seamen were sentenced to 6 months imprisonment for "having in their possessions Bolshevik literature", Cohen protested "if that is the extent of the liberty we have won from the War, it hardly seems worth getting." (8 February, 1920.)

Prosecutions for blasphemy re-appeared and Mr. Gott was a prime victim. Cohen, the National Secular Society, and the *Freethinker* frequently offered support to Gott in the various cases brought against him over several years, although Cohen did not approve of Gott's methods of propaganda which he considered too scurrilous and provocative: "And I must also say here that Mr. Gott by the methods he pursues, really plays into the hands of his persecutors... I do not say this by way of justifying or palliating his persecutors, but in these matters one ought to make up one's mind whether one desires to defeat blasphemy prosecutions or not." (13 February, 1921.)

Gott often preferred to defend himself and Cohen thought he did much harm to his own case and that of freethinkers by his muddled defence. The last blasphemy prosecution of an avowed freethinker was brought against Gott in 1921 and he was given nine months hard labour. He died a few weeks after serving the sentence. The N.S.S. organised a subscription to pay for Gott's appeal. There was public outcry at the severity of the sentence and impetus was given to the renewal of a campaign to abolish blasphemy laws.

Freethinkers thought it ludicrous that Christianity should be given special protection: "God, say the preachers aloud, lives in the hearts of his followers, to each other they whisper, 'but unless he is looked after by P.C. 342 the Lord help him and us.' " (13 February, 1921.)

Cohen's observations, after spending a morning in court at the time of one of Gott's trials, led him to sympathise with prison reform: "...the courts themselves are confederates with bad social conditions and defective education in the manufacturing of confirmed criminals." (13 February, 1921.)

The *Freethinker* also strongly criticised attempts to muzzle open-air speakers. Two examples about which the *Freethinker* displayed indignation were the fine of Guy Aldred for using insulting words in Hyde Park in 1925 and the police attempt to close a meeting of Len Ebury in North London at White Stone Pond, Hampstead, in 1936.

Aldred's offensive words included "Poor God, he wants the police here to be archangels, to work miracles to keep the crowd in order, and to do his work for him." (22 March, 1925.) Len Ebury faced rowdyism and disturbance from fascists and others, and the police wanted to close the meeting: "Mr. Ebury declined to have his meeting ended unless the police closed it by force. The speaker's firmness won the support of a number of those present and the meeting continued to its destined end." (2 February, 1936.)

Communications and Popular Culture

The failure of radio to become a form of communication open to all views was constantly bemoaned by the *Freethinker.* Specific attempts at censorship and control were, of course, condemned; for example, in 1936 J.B. Priestley was praised for refusing to send a manuscript of his talk to the BBC 14 days in advance of the broadcast. From the very beginnings of the wireless there was complaint at its use of sermons and church services, and its refusal to include freethought views. Cohen urged *Freethinker* readers to complain and roundly asked the BBC to cater for all views:

> The B.B.C. explained in a recent issue of its journal how popular its religious service on Sunday is. We have a suspicion that if many complaints had not been made about them there would not have been occasion for its attempted justification. For our part what has struck us about the sermons sent out by wireless is their unredeemed stupidity...
>
> "Someone has been writing to the *Manchester Guardian* protesting against the money raised from the taxation of wireless licences being used for this broadcasting of propaganda. At this the *Church Times* is vastly amused and explains that the B.B.C. tries to suit all tastes in the matter of religion as in all other things. Now that is simply not true. The B.B.C. merely tries to suit all *Christian* tastes... Religion should either be kept out of the wireless or views for and against should be permitted. (22 February, 1925.)

Reith, a Calvinist whose early control of the B.B.C. left an enduring mark was a favourite target. The *Freethinker* quoted Reith's views on religion and broadcasting put to a Government Committee considering the future of broadcasting: "There should be a definite association with religion in general and the Christian religion in particular. Broadcasting should not assist the secularization of Sunday." (13 December, 1925.)

Another developing medium of communication was the cinema film, and the churches quickly took advantage of their power and wealth, in a way quite beyond the resources of freethinkers, to expand their propaganda. A film "The Ten Commandments" was reviewed in the *Freethinker* and there was a note on a film "The History of the Vatican" to be shown by the Catholic Educational Company.

A news item reported an early example of a use of broadcasting which was to become characteristic of religion in America: the Paulist fathers intended to install a broadcasting station at the headquarters of their organisation, the Church of St. Paul the Apostle, New York, "for the purpose of acquainting the public with the Catholic point of view upon current affairs." (15 February, 1925.) Cohen doubted whether radio could effectively convey a religious message:

> But when the same prehistoric nonsense comes over the wireless to listeners lolling in easy chairs in front of a fire at home, where mundane sensible things surround them, it is, we fancy, apt to strike them as ridiculous... Whenever the Church advertises it must beware lest it rob religion of its atmosphere of mystery. Bring it down to the level of understandable things, and it is seen as the weird survival that it is. (8 February, 1925.)

He was perceptive in seeing the limitations of broadcast religion, but how wrong in underestimating the pervasiveness of religion upon the media, where lack of ideas and omnipresent vagueness are no disadvantage.

Popular culture, however, was showing a widely sceptical spirit and complete lack of concern for religious censure. An article on "Freethought in Unusual Places — The Revolutionary Kinema" took delight in Charlie Chaplin — "the prince of Kinema. Nothing is sacred to him. All the pomposities of life are mocked at and made a laughing-stock". (14 September, 1919.) A mention of jazz enlivens the sometimes dry columns of the *Freethinker;* when a French cardinal forbade dancing the tango, jazz, hesitation waltz, fox trot, and other new varieties of dance an Acid Drop item quipped "Our office boy declares this is the 'jazz-banned'." (4 January, 1920.)

The struggle to allow people to enjoy an entertaining Sunday continued. The Czech writer, Karel Capek, was quoted: "I do not know for what unutterable guilt the Lord has condemned England to the weekly punishment of Sunday". (3 May, 1925.) Petty controls were ridiculed: "In Sheffield, the Chief Constable has had the impudence to order that promoters of Sunday concerts shall submit their programmes to him for approval, so that this Jack-in-office may see that all are 'in keeping with the spirit of Sunday'..." (23 December, 1925.) The rationale of the Sunday Observance campaigners was punctured:

> The truth is that the only interest that is threatened by the secularizing of the day of rest is the interest of the clergy. And that rests upon sheer superstition... when in the course of time the Christian Church took over the day of the Sun, it transformed to it all the gloom of the day of Saturn (an early taboo). Here, as elsewhere, Christianity worsened almost all it touched. (15 February, 1920.)

The Continuing Criticism of Religion

The *Freethinker's* critical commentary on all religion remained sharp. The fundamentalist groups were the easiest target; the decline of traditional dogma by those who adhered to a vestigial Christianity was observed; the growth of the political influence of the Catholic Church was watched with concern; and new, sometimes bizarre, manifestations of religion were considered.

Among the evangelical groups the Salvation Army was constantly attacked for its money-making and crude faith. The Salvation Army's diamond jubilee in 1925 brought the opinion that "The country cannot be civilized, in the true sense of the word, while it has a Christian majority. Nor will matters be improved while Royal Persons, General Booth the Second, and his chocolate soldiers stand in adoration before a highly-coloured lithograph of a Saviour who never lived". (2 August, 1925.)

An earlier piece expanded upon a press exposure of the Salvation Army's finances, at a time when the Army was asking for half a million pounds in donations:

> They [the press] should inform their readers that the Army is a huge trading and commercial concern, that its help is sold to the poor, and that the food and shelter sold by such institutions as the Rowton Houses, and at such prices as yield a profit, gives much better value for money than do the Salvation Army shelters. They should tell their readers that the Army gets a commission on its emigration business, that it pays the poor social refuse that is driven to its worship a wage such as no firm would dare to offer them. (1 February, 1920.)

Arguments about a new prayer book and the Thirty-Nine-Articles showed Anglicanism in considerable confusion about its teaching. "What is Christianity?" became a relevant question, and Cohen, always quick to take up press discussion of religion, examined this question, which headed an article in the *Sunday Express:*

> What Christianity *is* it would puzzle anyone to say definitely... It means anything, everything, and nothing at all. It means in politics Socialism to one, Communism to another, Conservatism to another, and Liberalism to yet another. It means placing the next world first to this man, and last to that. It means exactly what anyone cares to make it. (11 January, 1925.)

When the House of Convocation discussed leaving our parts of the old prayer book, Cohen wrote: "Charles Bradlaugh, who was, in his way, a theologian, once said that religions do not die but they change... The ecclesiastics are getting nervous and are throwing out the sandbags in a frantic endeavour to escape the enemy sharpshooters". (19 July, 1925.) And he was amused at the suggestion that the Thirty-Nine-Articles might have to be abandoned because "there may be 'intellectual difficulties' on the part of aspirants to the clerical profession". (Ibid.)

In discussing the case of Bishop Barnes, who had been accused of heresy, Cohen suggested that it had shown "the hesitancy of leading men in the Christian Church to say precisely and definitely what it is a Christian ought to believe". He added that this indicated the advance of Freethought and "without conceit, much of this may be taken as a consequence of militant Freethought". (1 January, 1928.)

Cohen frequently opened the New Year with a general comment on the position of religion and freethought. In 1925 he wrote:

> The most powerfully organized religion in the world has been compelled to drop one doctrine after another, and to seek safety in vagueness even with those to which it still clings... The growth of avowed Freethought on the one hand, and the 'liberalizing' of religion on the other, has indeed gone on so rapidly that a great many have come apparently to the conclusion that it is unecessary to bother further, that the forces set in motion will of themselves sweep out of existence what remains of organised religious belief.

He added that the "Roman Catholic Church is gaining in political influence in this country, and there is a tendency on the part of politicians to pander to this or that group of organised religionists on account of the vote". He thought there was still a role for Freethought because "The world is riddled with insincerities and shams, and the greatest imposture of all is religion... Indifference is one of the most deadly enemies the reformer has to fight, and it is one of the best friends to all forms of obscurantism". (4 January, 1925.)

As the power of organised religion declined, the attack broadened to include obscurantism and superstition in general. The National Secular Society's A.G.M. in 1925 passed a motion which drew attention to the growing "prevalence of gross superstition among all classes of the community" at a time of "the rapid disintegration of orthodox Christianity."

The *Freethinker* has always contained entertaining accounts of some of the more way-out cults. An article entitled "Healthateria" by E.J. Lamel gave one such account:

> The other day I had put into my hand a bill announcing free lectures on "healthateria", by an American lady claiming to be a preceptress of "Super-Science", scientist, Christian psychologist, and Esoteric World Teacher. She has a peripatetic School of Cosmic (I had nearly omitted the 's' from that word) Science, Super-Psychology, Metaphysics, Divine Healing, Vocational Guidance, and Inspirational Development, where students are invited to learn (at a price) to solve the mysteries and secret teachings of Ancient Egypt, Greece, Persia, Chaldea, Assyria, Arabia and India; and since the Bible is an "occult book", the mysteries hidden therein.

The author attended the meeting at which the lady spoke:"It was entirely a plea for prayer instead of physic. The Lady claimed to have cured many things by the 'vibratory power of thought' from a distance. For example, a patient who had burst an artery was healed by this means... It was an ill-digested mixture of Christian Science, Theosophy, and mysticism ancient and modern..." He added that "This lady, incidentally, is holding classes in 'Super-Science Cookery', which my wife is attending, whether as a critic or student I do not yet know." His reason for writing on the matter was "to call the attention of Freethinkers to these freak cults which are in competition with conventional religion, and are even more insidious in fostering forms of superstition very difficult to eradicate." (22 April, 1928.)

Numerous articles in the *Freethinker* dealt with the history of Christianity and of Freethought, examined the Bible and the historicity of Jesus, and explored the sociology of religion. "The Meanderings of a Sceptic" was a title which would have been appropriate for many articles. "I do not think that any propagandist need apologise for being guilty of re-iteration", wrote Cohen in a front page article on freethought propaganda. (7 June, 1925.) However, Cohen was culpable, and there is no denying the repetitiousness of some of his writing. In mitigation it may be said that there was clearly a continued audience of readers to whom the basic questioning of the tenets of religion and Christianity was new. Justifying the repetition of fundamental points, T.H. Ebstrob wrote:

> Plugging may be abhorrent, but the lesson that there are some truths so important that they need constant repetition is an educational commonplace that must not be neglected. Because *Constant Reader* has read *ad nauseam* in our columns that professional followers of the Carpenter who preached Hell for the Rich, dwell in Palaces, dress sumptuously and eat with gusto, it does not mean that the point does not need constant re-emphasis. (25 July, 1937.)

The debate between religion and science was still seen as important. Although scientific detail was not included in a journal intended for the general reader, scientific materialism and evolution were two of Cohen's major themes. There was a general condemnation of famous scientists who added weight to religion by association rather than by argument — Sir Oliver Lodge and James Jeans were criticised for this. When Lodge preached in Purley Congregational Church, Cohen wrote:

> What the religionist loves to dwell upon is not the conquests of science but its failures. He is happiest when he is able to say that science cannot explain this or that. It is not science but nescience that he loves... Ignorance is a field on which the fool and the philosopher are on an equality — and the fool knows it... Unfortunately these aberrations are not new by any means. We have had Sir Isaac Newton on prophecies and we have had Michael Faraday among the Sandemanians. (15 March, 1925.)

Cohen was extremely interested in materialism, about which he wrote a book, and criticised Eddington's *The Nature of the Physical World* because it contained the suggestion that the new physics gave grounds for an idealistic philosophy which "is hospitable towards a spiritual religion". Eddington paid Cohen the compliment of writing a detailed reply for publication in the *Freethinker* in which he called Cohen "a fair-minded opponent". (20 October, 1929.)

The Scopes trial in Tennessee in 1925 was regarded as evolution on trial. John Scopes was a biology teacher in Dayton, Tennessee, who was accused of teaching the theory of evolution in defiance of a Tennessee State Law forbidding the theory from being included in school lessons. William Jennings Bryan, a leading fundamentalist and a former Presidential candidate, assisted the state prosecution and the American Civil Liberties Union supported Scopes. Scopes was found guilty and fined, but the freethinking lawyer Clarence Darrow, who defended him, was the intellectual victor. Bryan collapsed and died — as did most of the anti-evolution case. British bishops said the Tennessee fundamentalists were behind the times, but Cohen condemned their hypocrisy.

> The people of Dayton have been trying to show us what getting back to the real Jesus means. The Bishop of Durham and all those who are more concerned with concealing the nature of religion than they are with preaching it, do not like it. As a Freethinker I thank them. I prefer honest ignorance to sophisticated and time-serving knowledge. (16 August, 1925.)

The *Freethinker* highlighted the hypocrisy of "advanced Christians" who were "poking fun at the Christians of Dayton" while ignoring similar cases in England. An example was that of a schoolteacher in Bootle who had taught girls the theory of evolution and the mythical nature of the Adam and Eve story and was told by the education committee to "train scholars in the habits of reverence towards God and religion." (9 August, 1925.) Further American anti-evolution incidents were reported: books dealing with evolution were sought and burnt in a public bonfire at Southern Junior College, Cooltma, and the renowned *Webster's Dictionary* was banished from all public libraries and institutions in Little Rock, Arkansas, because of the anti-evolution law.

In England, freethinkers continued to campaign to secularise teaching about religion in school. Harry Snell, a staunch secularist, later to be elevated to the House of Lords and become Under-Secretary for India, was Secretary of the Secular Education League. In 1920, there were fears that the Education Minister, H.A.L. Fisher, would strengthen religious instruction in schools as "a species of backstairs trafficking". (18 April, 1920.) Teachers were thought to be pusillanimous in their failure to oppose R.I. and Cohen summed up an NUT conference in 1931 with the headline "Teachers as Parsonic Cats-paws". (19 April, 1931.)

The Church lobbies, demanding more financial support for church schools, were strengthened. A Roman Catholic campaign at the time of the 1931 Education Act (which raised the school leaving age) urged an Amendment giving more funds to Church schools:

> Special sermons were given, and its followers were supplied with forms of letters and cards wherewith to bombard Members of Parliament, and threaten them with the combined opposition of the Catholic vote unless an amendment was passed to the effect that the new Education Act should not become operative until the extra expense entailed on non-provided schools was made good from public funds and with no increase of public control. (1 February, 1931.)

An aspect of the churches' political involvement which was strongly ridiculed was that of Christian Socialism. Maybe freethinkers were incensed that Christians should try to take over their own radical pitch. Foote had predicted that "the parsons will nobble the Socialist movement", and an article on "Socialism and Religion" observed this happening: "The practice of Idealism or Altruism, without belief in the Incarnation, is, according to Father Bull of the Church Socialist league, doomed to utter failure and disaster." The *Freethinker* naturally disagreed, seeing idealism and altruism as a "perfectly natural and rational outcome of circumstances, heredity and environment..." (30 May, 1920.) Mimnermus was scathing about the clergy "making love to Democracy":

> The purse-proud prelates of the Government Religion have actually arranged a 'Labour Service' at Southwark Cathedral; and the President of the Free Church Council, the Rev. F.B. Meyer, who is old enough to know better, declares that "the axioms of the Labour party" were first uttered by Jesus Christ... The present-day hypocritical pretensions of the clergy are nauseating. (4 April, 1920.)

A rare example of humorous verse depicts "The Socialist Parson":

> Let's talk of wages, hours, and food,
>   And the rights and wrongs of labour;
> Of Marx, monopoly, surplus wealth.
>   But please don't mention the Saviour.
> ......
> Just here me orate on the Socialist State,
>   When life will be leisure and roses.
> I preach without ruth all Socialist truth
>   But not the mistakes of Moses.
>
> Then brothers, my brothers, arise and unite
>   Around the dear flag which is red,
> And get all you can according to plan,
>   For perhaps when we die we are dead.
>
> G.P. (13 June, 1920.)

When the Pope condemned socialism in 1925, Cohen asked: "We wonder how many thousands of Catholic supporters of the English Labour Party think of this, and how they will act." (4 January, 1925.) And in the following issue he ridiculed Christian socialism:

> The theory of "our brother Christ" will not do. The New Testament drama was not written, the Christian roll of martyrs was not compiled, sects have not been formed, the fires of Smithfield have not burned, nor were the tortures of inquisitions perpetrated in order to secure better hours of labour, more wages, or the municipalization of this or that. (11 January, 1925.)

Brother Christ was not much in evidence to clasp the hand of the working man at the time of the General Strike, and the Churches prayed for peace. The Christian editor of the *Sunday Express*, James Douglas, wrote that prayer "enabled us to pull through the General Strike." Cohen disagreed:

> If Mr. Douglas showed any capacity for seeing to the roots of affairs he might reflect that the Great Strike exemplified, not the power of prayer, but the strength of the social consciousness and the capacity of human nature to work for an ideal... The real and enduring lesson of the Strike is the enormous capacity of human nature for right action, once it is properly educated and widely directed. More than ever one feels it is not an

> emphasis on the sickly sentimentality of 'Christian love' that the world needs, but on the Freethought message of enlightenment and wise direction. (23 May, 1926.)

The political influence of the clergy in the House of Lords was deplored, "because the Bench of Bishops in the Upper Chamber forms the last stronghold of Ecclesiasticism in this country..." A move from the Conservative party to reform the House of Lords was seen as

> A very effective piece of camouflage which requires the close attention of all who have the cause of Democracy at heart... The House of Lords has suddenly become aware of the impending conflict (as a result of Labour reform proposals) and is trying to bamboozle the official Labour Party, which, in view of Mr. Ramsay MacDonald's admiration for royalty, and Mr. Henderson's fulsome piety, may not be an altogether impossible problem... Real Democrats must see to it that the House of Lords is abolished, and not merely re-upholstered. (30 December, 1928.)

Politics and the Monarchy

The *Freethinker* rarely commented on party politics, but after the election of a National Government in 1931 Cohen wrote a front-page article, belying the usual disclaimer with which he began:

> We are not concerned with the partizan implications of the General Election. We regret that in the deluge more than one good friend of Freethought has been put out of action in the Parliamentary field... We fear that it [the new Government] will be more concerned to avoid collisions on matters on which opinion is divided upon party lines, than to use its disproportionate majority to deal with some matters which do not come into that category. In any case no Government can do worse than the late Labour Government did in its action with regard to the Blasphemy Act, the Sunday Performances Bill and its own Education Bill. The surrender of the latter to sectarian clamour, and that by a Labour Government, which, when most of its members were propagandists, had secular education in its programme, is as good evidence as any reasonable person could require of the folly of associating our movement with the opportunists of any Party. (8 November, 1931.)

Few politicians were praised by the *Freethinker,* but Baldwin was singled out for especial condemnation. When he addressed the "Empire Youth" at the Albert Hall, Cohen wrote:

> That speech was very Baldwinian. It contained much that his hearers would not clearly understand, much that might be all right if one took it in a sense different from that which Mr. Baldwin intended, and much that meant nothing. And some of it would have been worthy of the Archbishop of Canterbury with whom Mr. Baldwin has been in such truly Christian agreement ever since the affair of Edward VIII. (30 May, 1937.)

Always a republican paper, the *Freethinker* was given opportunity for rich comment at the time of the constitutional crisis provoked by Edward VIII's decision to marry Mrs. Simpson. Some commentators had suggested that the marriage ought to be morganatic, so that the children could not inherit, but the *Freethinker* saw no reason why Mrs. Simpson's children should be any less suitable than those of previous monarchs:

> We have had within the past century and a half, a stupid monarch, an obstinate, fussy and prejudiced monarch, and the British Empire has managed to come into existence and survive. It is not likely, then, that in the event of the monarchy continuing through Edward the Eighth and Mrs. Simpson, anything very disastrous will happen. (13 December, 1936.)

Freethinkers thought Edward VIII should "insist on his right to marry whom he pleases":

> Let us hope that the King has among his subjects a sufficiently large number of healthy-minded men and women to appreciate the painful position in which both he and Mrs. Simpson are placed by law and customs based on primitive ideas of Kingship; and also that a much larger number of men and women have enough healthy romance in their make-up to feel for a man and a woman who are obviously linked together in terms of real and deep affection. (Ibid.)

Cohen was interested in rumours concerning the King's religious orthodoxy, and wrote that he was said to have raised objections to the religious aspect of the accession oath "although his objection, if it existed, was finally overcome."

Two key factors were seen as the collusion of Baldwin and the Archbishop of Canterbury, Lang, and the Church of England's bitter opposition to relaxation of the Divorce Laws. Cohen cheekily suggested that the couple should do away with the religious ceremony altogether and use a Register Office. "There would be such a boom in marriage before a Registrar that the Church would almost lose the whole of its profitable trade in weddings, with all that it implies in the shape of breeding new customers for its semi-magical business."

Cohen thought the King was "sacrificed to religious intolerance and political chicanery". He abhorred the spectacle of the media and people transferring their allegiance from Edward VIII to George VI:

> Five months of intensive, and expensive, advertising of the graciousness of the Queen, the beauty of the children, the happiness of the Royal Family, and the devotion of George the Sixth to duty, will do the trick... The men who marched down Whitehall waving penny flags shouting "We want Edward" will be waving the same flags and shouting "We've got George"... (20 December, 1936.)

Dictatorship and Authoritarianism

Between the first and second world wars a growing theme was the growth of dictatorship and authoritarianism. As early as 1925, Cohen wrote: "All over the world there has been a tremendous growth in the principle of mere authority. The war accentuated it but other forces have played their part... The Freethought party is the only one in this country that is prepared to stand for freedom of thought and expression, whether it agrees with the opinions expressed or not. And that is the only assertion of freedom worth anything". (6 December, 1925.) Between the Russian Revolution and the rise of Hitler, the *Freethinker*, which had not traditionally devoted a great deal of space to international affairs, steadily increased its coverage of conflicts between nations.

The *Freethinker* was eventually neutral towards the Bolshevik transformation of Russian society, and Cohen said of the re-organisation of Russian society on "something of a Communistic Basis" — "That is a form of Government to which many would object, ourselves among the number". (23 November, 1919.) However, there had initially been some enthusiasm for a revolution which was seen as a blow to the Christian Church as well as Russian autocracy: "the makers of the revolution were, and are, in the main Freethinkers. The greatest figure of all at the moment, Trotsky — the man who is responsible for giving an idea to the peoples of the world around which they may rally — is an avowed Freethinker... They [the revolutionaries] appeal to the peoples of the world against the rulers of the world, to human reason against brute force. And that appeal has brought the world nearer peace than has three-and-a-half years fighting". (10 February, 1918.)

A frequent comment in the twenties was related to the Churches' attempts to use the Russian revolution to discredit freethought. The *Freethinker* queried the press attempts to show all Russian changes in their worst light: "What is the exact truth about Russia we cannot say... From the situation two things seem clear. The first is, that some lying of the very tallest order is going on. Our atrocity mills have been working at full pressure, and the most incredible stories have been accepted on the very slenderest of evidence. Secondly, the Soviet Government does appear to have made some attempt to reorganize Russian Society on something of a Communistic basis. Such a re-organisation included a sweeping attack on established religion:

> They have cleared religion out of State offices and out of schools. They appear to be making a more serious attempt than is being made anywhere else in Europe to give every child a good education *minus* religion. And all the Churches everywhere are alarmed. They see the chance of killing two birds with one stone. By dwelling upon the evils of Bolshevism, and upon the way in which its leaders oppose religion, they can help the Church in Russia and discountenance Freethought at home... Tyranny may exist in the absence of religious help; but there is no other assistance that can so well perpetuate its being. (23 November, 1919.)

The rise of fascism and the coming to power of Mussolini were seen as dangerous trends, and the Concordat between Mussolini and the Pope was vigorously condemned. The *Church Times* thought an article in the *Daily Express* describing "the special form of Bolshevik tyranny carried on in Italy under Mussolini" was "overdone", because "Mussolini has not shed the blood of priests and bishops as the rulers of Russia have done." Cohen wrote sarcastically — "That does of course make a tremendous difference. The murder of ordinary people who venture to criticize a dictatorship that is in alliance with the Holy Roman Church, may be excusable but the killing of the Lord's appointed is a thing that no good Christian can overlook." (25 October, 1925.)

Eleven years later Italy conquered Abyssinia:

> Italy will now in the name of civilization — Christian civilization — assume control over Abyssinia, and the business of the 'Powers' will be to devise some formula that will look as though right and justice demand that Italy shall have her way.
>
> Our own Minister of War, recently declared that every branch of the Christian Church agreed that the army was a noble profession. Not a necessary profession or a profession that we must submit to with all the evil consequences that an army must bring, for a sectional army can live only on mutual distrust of others and the expectancy of war, from which it follows that war itself is also noble — but a "noble profession"! Well, Italy has at least given us a sample of what the noble profession is capable of. Aeroplanes showering mustard gas on women and children, dropping poison gas and explosive bombs on hordes of men unable even to strike back, blasting collections of mud huts off the face of the earth, and firing on hospitals whenever the occasion offered... (12 April, 1936.)

The Spanish revolution and subsequent civil war were closely watched by the *Freethinker.* The replacement of the Spanish King Alfonso by a Republic in 1931 was viewed with optimism, although there were fears that it would be used to discredit atheists just as the Bolshevik revolution had been. The Republic planned to limit clerical powers and secularise education, but the Archbishop of Toledo warned that the Church would not surrender any of its rights. Cohen observed:

> No one who remembers what are the claims of the Church, even in this country, will be in any doubt as to what this means in such a country as Spain. The Roman Church everywhere says quite plainly that an education that is not permeated with its teaching is not education at all. In Italy it has protested against Protestants being permitted to carry on their propaganda, and has charged Mussolini with a breach of the Concordat. In Spain it is protesting against anything of the kind being allowed there. (31 May, 1931.)

When riots broke out after a peaceful revolution, Cohen suggested that they had been fomented by opponents of the revolution to bring it into disrepute: "This it may be pointed out is an old trick in Spain." He recalled the "outrages" at the time of Ferrer's execution, which were "fomented and carried out by some religious orders." (31 May, 1931.)

A manifesto from Rome to the Spanish Government demanded "restoration of the privileges and powers of the Spanish Church as they existed previous to the deposition of Alfonso," and the *Freethinker* commented that "The Roman Church represents the menace of religion to civilization in its most complete form." (5 July, 1931.)

As the Civil War developed, it was noted that "the *Daily Mail* is still working hard, backed up by the Roman Catholics, to convert the Civil War in Spain into a new religious crusade, and continues to fight against Atheism and anti-Christianity." (30 August, 1936.) Links between fascism and Catholicism were seen:

> ...it is well to remember that the Roman Catholic Church is openly allied with Fascism in Italy; and in Spain, is backing the Fascist rebellion against the Government. In Germany it is not openly supporting the most beastly form of Fascism in existence, simply because Fascism there will not give to the Roman Catholic Church the privileges that is given it under Mussolini. (Ibid.)

Cohen thought that "All war is brutalizing and tends to degradation" but with the war in Spain "the crowning act of brutality" was the destruction of Guernica:

> This was an open town. It was not inhabited by Atheistic 'Reds', no Churches had been destroyed; the people were very strongly Roman Catholic. But relay after relay of German planes flew over the place, flying as low as they pleased, so that there could be no difficulty in reaching their mark. The town was completely destroyed, and the women and children were followed up by planes, and machine-gunned as they tried to escape over open fields... Publicity for this tremendous crime was too much even for Franco & Co. They deny having anything to do with it. Germany also issued the same denial, so did Italy, although no one but Baldwin, Simon, Hoare and Eden, would place the slightest reliance upon the word of either Hitler or Mussolini. We are to suppose that it was the Government itself that destroyed Guernica and massacred its inhabitants. Is it any wonder that people fly before the advance of rebels as from the plague? (9 May, 1937.)

There was equally strong condemnation of the Home Secretary's ungenerous attitude to the reception of child refugees: John Simon was "willing to allow a limited number of children to come to England, provided that the funds in the hands of the relief committee are adequate to cover the expense of each child brought here, and that no charge is incurred by public funds for their maintenance. I question whether anything meaner has ever occurred in the history of this country... Are we to believe that there is any considerable body of people in Britain who would begrudge, say, a farthing rate for the feeding of these little victims of Fascist brutality?... Sir John professes to be a follower of one who is reported to have said, 'Suffer little children to come unto me,' and Simon adds to the text the proviso, 'But they may come only in small numbers, and must not become a charge on public funds.' " (9 May, 1937.)

The *Freethinker* consistently opposed Nazism and highlighted the political persecution taking place in Germany. The appeals for help for refugees were seen to symbolise religious divisiveness:

> We have received a copy of "The National Christian Appeal" on behalf of the refugee Christian victims of Hitlerism. The purpose is a good one, and nothing that anyone can say can overcolour the tortures to which children, women and old men are subjected in Hitler's Germany — a country to which our Government, through the King, recently sent birthday greetings with best wishes for the prosperity of Hitler...
>
> But the pity of it! There are appeals to Jews to help the Jewish Victims of Hitlerism. There are appeals to Christians to help the Christian victims of

> Hitlerism. Each one appeals to, and so helps to keep alive, the very thing that provides the victims on whose behalf help is asked. It is the religious spirit, Jewish, Christian, or other, that has kept alive the spirit of persecution from which these helpless people are suffering. Hitler's crime is not fundamentally against Jew or Christian, but against *humanity*. (17 May, 1936.)

The rise of Hitlerism was seen to have historical causes and to have parallels with religion:

> Germany under Hitler has had the doubtful honour of embracing a new religion. Like every new religion it is only a rehash of old ideas in a new form. It is the new religion of the State Supreme, founded to control the destiny of the German people chosen by God, Nature, and Hitler, to rule the world.
>
> ...Hitler is a product of the Versailles Treaty. That disgraceful pact made Hitler's rise possible. The feeling of bitterness and resentment which filled the German people with burning desire to revenge themselves overshadowed all other considerations. It fanned the flames of Nationalism, and eventually overthrew the mild Socialist Government. ("Race, Religion and Nationalism" by Idris Llewellyn Abraham.) (16 February, 1936.)

One bias which the *Freethinker* was happy to be accused of was bias against fascism:

> A correspondent charges us with being "heavily biased against Fascism". Of course we have a "bias" against Fascism, as we have a bias for or against many other things... A Fascist who is forbidden to listen to the other side, and where Fascism is in power, is punished if he does, strikes us as the last word in human degradation. And we continue to be "heavily biased" against such a system — if "system" is not too dignified a name for it. (16 August, 1936.)

Cohen, who was himself from a Jewish background, saw the persecution of Jews as a religious problem and a part of the Christian tradition. He had always opposed the creation of a Jewish state in Palestine, because it would create a religious state and perpetuate the Judaic religious identity. In 1919 he wrote an article entitled "The Myth of the Jew": "They are no more a nation than are Freemasons or Roman Catholics." As far as Jews had anything in common, in Cohen's view, it was religion — which was preserved by Christian persecution. Insofar as persecution of Jews continued and they needed sanctuary, "The reason is political or humanitarian and does not at all rest on the question of nationality." "Does the world really desire to see another religious State set up? ...as Christianity weakens so will Judaism disappear. It has been kept alive by Christianity, and the world will be the better for the disappearance of both." (30 March, 1919.)

This opinion was repeated in 1931, with the emphasis that a Jewish religious state could itself display intolerance:

> One of the avowed, but not of course the real, reasons for the settlement of the Jews in Palestine was to remove them from the persecution of bigoted

> Christians. But it is quite certain that Jews, so long as they remain true to their religion will be as ready to persecute as ever Christians were. From the *Jewish Chronicle* we learn that there was some rioting in Palestine owing to one lot of Jews trying to prevent another lot from playing football on the Sabbath. Really religious people never learn toleration from experiencing persecution, they are only more anxious to prove that they can be as intolerant as their persecutors. (28 June, 1931.)

Such a view in no way justified European anti-Semitism and the *Freethinker* deplored the British fascists' utter contempt for free speech and human rights. A meeting of "Sir Oswald Mosley and his army of gallant blackshirts" was referred to; mention of Jews produced "howls and roars of exultant hatred" and Mr. William Hickey, at the press table for the *Daily Express*, commented after being evicted, that "I have been present at many scenes of violence, but I don't think that I have ever heard such bestially savage cries and yells." (26 March, 1939.)

The Oxford Group's sympathy for fascism was also described as "as fine a specimen of religious ignorance and cheap emotionalism as one could wish." (13 September, 1936.) The *Freethinker* reported:

> Mr. Frank Buchman has been carrying his Gospel into America. There he is reported as saying, "Thank God for Adolf Hitler for building a strong bulwark against a Godless Russia. If only Mr. Hitler would become a first-century Christian, Europe would be completely saved." (4 October, 1936.)

Bigotry and cruel intolerance in America were described in an article on "The Religion of the 'Klu-Klux-Klan' " by George Bedborough. The Klu-Klux-Klan — "a synonym for fanatical gangsterism" — were also known as the Black Legion: "The immediate victims the Black Legion are fighting are negroes, Catholics and Freethinkers." (6 September, 1936.)

The *Freethinker* was an early opponent of racism. At the time of the Amritsar massacre in India, during which there was wholesale slaughter of unarmed citizens by the British, any idea of white superiority was forthrightly condemned:

> The Secretary of State for India was almost quoting from a paragraph in this column of a week or so ago when he said there was a theory abroad that an Indian "is a person who is tolerable as long as he obeys your orders." That, we think, is the attitude of the white man generally towards the coloured races — black, brown, and yellow — all the world over... The Christian interpretation of the brotherhood of man has never been allowed to interfere with it. (18 July, 1920.)

A similar limit to Christian belief in the Brotherhood of Man was seen in South Africa. The *Freethinker* picked up a report in the *Rand Mail* of a member of the Dutch Reformed Church who made a savage attack on Church of England parsons who had been championing the natives: "He said that South Africa's two greatest dangers were Communists and the English parsons." He wanted "absolute segregation" and the *Freethinker* in speaking of the Kaffirs retorted ironically — "Evidently

God blundered when he made them." (13 December, 1925.)

Freethinkers were themselves persecuted in parts of Europe in the 1930s. An article by C. Bradlaugh Bonner reported developments among European freethinkers. The Freethought Federation, often known as the Brussels Federation, because it was initiated in Brussels in 1880, was reformed as the World Union of Freethinkers because of arguments about the extent of its political affiliations. Bradlaugh Bonner wrote:

> The formation of the World Union of Freethinkers has fluttered more than one dove-cote. It has led in Poland to the prohibition of Freethought associations. In Holland and Belgium the Catholic newspapers have hurled at it a stream of abuse, endeavouring to curdle the blood of their readers... In Italy, Germany, Austria, Poland, Roumania, Lithuania, Latvia, Esthonia and Bulgaria, Freethought is banned. Yet the Pansy[1]) grows hidden in secret places despite the Crutched Cross, the Swastika and the Axe. (15 November, 1936.)

Parallel to Cohen's comment on the growth of authoritarianism during the inter-war years ran his disappointment that the popular press had failed to develop mankind's capacity for reason and his fear that the manufacture of mass opinion was creating conformity of behaviour. Perhaps his view of the popular press was soured by the *Freethinker's* failure to reach a mass audience, but his criticism has a serious point:

> If the press had risen to its opportunities for good, all would have been well. But has it? What it has seen is the opportunity of larger and larger circulations, the condition of obtaining which has been to play to ignorance rather than to work for its removal. Stunts — whether it is the daily movements of an evangelist like Mrs. McPherson, or the elaborate chronicling of a murder trial — are the order of the day. Pictures, which for their sheer inanity almost defy description, take up a large part of the space available. The leading article is fast disappearing to make room for short paragraphs which call for no mental effort on the part of the reader. And even that is apparently too much, for in most cases the news has to be given in headlines, for fear the average reader should find the strain of even a thirty line paragraph too much, for his, or her, intelligence...
>
> It is only a paper such as the *Freethinker* which makes sales a secondary consideration, and the consequence is chronic poverty. (21 October, 1928.)

The production of conformist opinions by schools and the press could endanger freethought as much as the more straightforward indoctrination of the Churches:

> In all these matters, and in the presence of actual events we are faced with the production of mass opinion as a desirable end in life. It is taken as an essential task of "leaders of opinion" to create it. Again the conviction is general. With the Church it has always been an obvious aim. To get the whole population to sing the praise of the blood of Jesus in the same words, to the same tune, and with the same meaning — or lack of meaning — is the religious ideal. To get the whole of the people acclaiming a blind support of "god and King" is the ideal of the old-fashioned Conservative.

[1]) The Pansy was a symbol of freethought, perhaps related to the French word *pensée*.

> And to suppress all opinions but one, and to unite all in the worship of certain economic theories in precisely the same language is the ideal of the genuine Communist. A Society in which all men and women shall say the same things, and profess belief in the same things marks the triumph of mass production in the world of intelligence, and it is a danger far graver than anything else that confronts us at present. We are killing religion in the churches only to resurrect it in social life. (22 November, 1931.)

However, the most serious threat, as Cohen made clear at the beginning of 1939, was authoritarianism:

> The main principle on which Freethought rests is now challenged over a large part of the world, and in some countries independent thinking has again become one of the most serious crimes. Slave States (it is more euphonius to call them 'Authoritarian' or 'Totalitarian' States, although both terms stand for States in which the individual possesses no rights whatever with regard to freedom of movement, speech, thought, or publication) exist and even in this country we have many people in high places, and holding Government positions, who hardly trouble to show their deep sympathy with these servile States. "National necessity" is a phrase that goes far with these people as a means of fooling others, and the issue of war or peace is placed before an unthinking public when the real issue is that of war, and something even worse than war. We have again to reargue positions and principles that were fifty years ago generally accepted. (1 January, 1939.)

CHAPTER V
THE SECOND WORLD WAR AND POST-WAR PERIOD

"The Armistice of 1918-39 is at an end. Since 11 o'clock on September 3 this country has been at war with Germany, and if ever war was justifiable it is the one in which this country is now engaged." (10 September, 1939.) Although the *Freethinker* had always abhorred militarism, it was almost with a sense of relief that Cohen wrote of the declaration of war against Hitler. He had earlier written that the choice was not between peace and war but between war and something worse: "The present conflict, which may or may not end in war, is not a conflict between two nations or between two groups of nations. It is a fight for the maintenance of even the moderately decent level of life that has been achieved." (30 April, 1939.)

Cohen did not share illusions, soon to be nurtured by British propaganda, that the allies possessed a moral superiority or that the war was caused solely by the evil genius of one dictator. In writing of a justifiable war a few months before the declaration of hostilities, Cohen explained that "I do not mean by this that the hands of this country are spotless"; "on the contrary, there are some very nasty spots on our hands, and these spots will not be easily erased. After all, it was Britain that in modern times set the standard of national greatness as consisting mainly in vast 'possessions' in all parts of the globe, and so ultimately made it necessary for other powers to break the peace of Europe if they were to become 'great' powers also." (30 April, 1939.)

Opposing "the theory that war is the product of one man's activity", Cohen wrote:

> Such men as Hitler are the scum that society may throw to the surface, and it should be treated as a cook treats scum in the cooking — it should be thrown on one side as soon as noticed. In life events explained men, and the origin of the criminal gang against which we are now fighting is in the world they found established. (17 September, 1939.)

Attitudes to War

Some of Foote's articles from the First World War were reprinted as relevant comment on the repetition of man's inhumanity to man. And some of the same themes were to be repeated in the *Freethinker*: the uselessness of days of prayer and the impossibility of believing in a benevolent god during wartime, the rights of atheists to affirm and to opt out of church parade, the position of conscientious objectors, the need to avoid as much censorship as possible despite the demands of propaganda, the inanity of assuming all Germans were cruel monsters.

Innumerable comments were written about national days of prayer. They were compared to magical dances performed by medicine men when tribes go to war. What could be the use of prayer? "Was it intended to call God's attention to the fact that there is a war on, and give him a polite reminder that we expect him to do something?" (15 October, 1939.) An Acid Drop parodied Churchill in printing "What the Archbishop of Canterbury did *not* say on the National Day of Prayer. — Never has so little been done by *One*, for so few." (30 March, 1939.) Lord Halifax, Foreign Secretary, asked the public to form prayer groups and to spend a portion of each day in prayer: "Bearing in mind the opinions of large numbers of men in the British forces, a more disgraceful exhibition of using a public position to conduct a Christian propaganda has seldom been heard." (28 July, 1940.)

There was indignation at the difficulties encountered by atheists who wished to affirm rather than swear an oath of loyalty when they joined the forces. Freethinker readers were regularly informed of their rights and asked to report examples of discrimination. Two examples are typical. An individual wrote a letter recounting his experience of being sworn in for service in the RAF:

> On the form I had to fill in, opposite the words "Religious Denomination" I had written that I was an Atheist, although the recruiting officer had advised me to write "Church of England". When the attestation officer saw this he endeavoured to get me to change it to one of the recognized religions, and said that I must have a religion. When I asked him why I should have a religion he did not answer, and I am afraid to say that he was not at all sure how an Atheist had to be sworn in. I told him that he would have to change the words "Almighty God" in the oath, and that I could attest by affirmation, by my own integrity. He replied by saying that an Atheist couldn't have any integrity. Perhaps you can guess my reaction to this piece of unprecedented "cheek". I told him that an Atheist had more integrity than a Christian could ever have, because an Atheist used common sense in being what he was. Furthermore, I let him know that an Atheist had the integrity to be not afraid to stick to his principles in the face of all intimidation and opposition, and that whatever trouble I had to put up with in the R.A.F. I would continue to stick by them, and not insult them by telling lies for the sake of a lot of red tape and hypocrisy. (29 October, 1939.)

Another reader sent in a succinct recollection of what had happened when he had enlisted in the previous World War:

> The officer is taking down particulars at the Recruiting Office:—
> Officer: "Religion?"
> I: "None."
> (The officer writes "Church of England".)
> I: "I say 'No religion' and you write 'Church of England'."
> Officer: "Same thing." Then, after a pause: "Young man, if you want to kill someone, you must have a religion." (18 October, 1942.)

Protest also came as a result of the unpleasant fatigue duties, such as cleaning the lavatories, which were given to those who opted out of the Army Church Parade. The provision of Bibles for service men and women, with a message from the King urging Bible reading, was seen as insulting to a force that contained Mohammedans, Buddhists and unbelievers:

> All are asked to believe that the book which kept religious persecution alive, which taught the belief in witchcraft, which sanctioned slavery, which taught exorcism as a method of curing disease, which told women they were to obey their husbands with the same unquestioning obedience that they obeyed Jesus Christ, the book which substantially ignores the family, which has nothing to say concerning art, science, education, philosophy, and which out-Nazied Nazi brutality with its doctrine of eternal damnation, it is this book that has been "a wholesome and strengthening influence in our national life". (15 October, 1939.)

The *Freethinker* strongly objected to the view that the war was "being fought for the preservation of Christianity" (25 August, 1940.) and to attempts by the churches to capitalise on the grim situation. "The Government at the opening of the war avowed its determination to prevent profiteering. But it probably did not interfere with the greatest of all forms of profiteering, that of the Christian Church... we may say that the exploitation of human fear and ignorance in the interests of superstition begins with the earliest and persists with the latest forms of religion." (8 September, 1940.)

Strong distaste for warmongering and any Christian relish for war was registered:

> Mr. Winston Churchill said: "We will make them [the Germans] bleed and burn." As the Daring Old Man on the Flying Trapeze of the war, jumping from Turkey to Casablanca, Winston has said something of which millions of Christians have heartily approved. It is a thoroughly Christian sentiment in line with Christian history and Christian traditions — far more so than when Winston said, "War is an evil thing." (28 March, 1943.)

Duff Cooper suggested that "there is some profound quality that differentiates the Germans from other people". Cohen dealt with such a view with the same anti-mystical, sociological approach that he brought to religion. He quoted J.S. Mill: "Of all the vulgar modes of escaping from the consideration of the effect of social and moral influence on the human mind, the most vulgar is that of attributing the diversities of conduct and character to inherent natural differences." Cohen continued:

> From my youth upwards it has been plain to me that while there may be different endowments with individuals, so that some Germans may be as independent in their outlook as some Englishmen, and some Englishmen as sheep-like in their mentality as some Germans, it is the social and cultural environment in which we find ourselves that is responsible for the forms of expression of those qualities that are common to all. (29 October, 1939.)

Comment in the *Freethinker* in the thirties had compared fascism and Nazism to the phenomenon of religions. A report of the plan of Rosenberg, the "German 'racial' expert with a Jewish name", to replace the Bible by *Mein Kampf* highlighted a religious component of Nazism:

> *Mein Kampf* is to take the place of the Bible in German Churches. The State Church is to be anti-Atheistic and one in which all German men and

> women, youths and girls "acknowledge God and his eternal works." The matter is interesting because, first it disproves the religious talk of Hitler and his gang being all Atheists — they are, as a matter of fact, mainly religious. Next it shows that in the attempt to enslave Germans perpetually the gang can find no better implement than religion, and thirdly, in establishing a National Church where only one form of religious belief is permitted, Hitler and his gang are pilfering the ideal of the Roman Church, and, indeed, of every established Church in Christendom. The brutalities of Hitlerism should not blind intelligent people to these pregnant facts. (14 December, 1941.)

Hitler was as fickle and opportunist in his attitude to churches as to any other group. He was originally Catholic, but although some parts of the Catholic Church had shown sympathy for fascist elements, it would be as wrong to brand Hitler as a puppet of any church, as to assign his evils to any atheism. Cohen was asked to justify his rather ambivalent statement that Hitler was a "deeply religious man" and he quoted an early utterance of Hitler's from the "sixpenny *Hammer and Anvil*": "I believe it was God's will to send out a boy from here into the Reich to make him great, to raise him to be Fuehrer of the nation, to enable him to lead his homeland back to the Reich. There is a higher dispensation and we are nothing but its instruments..." (13 August, 1939.)

A complete and judicious assessment of the relationship between Nazism, Hitler and religion would need more space than is available here, but it would have to include reference to some Christians' courageous resistance to Nazism as well as Pius XII's failure actively to condemn Nazism.

If churches could debase the epithet "atheist" by attaching it to Nazi rulers, they were presented with problems when atheistic Russia became an ally. The picture established in the twenties and thirties had to be reversed: "The picture of Russia as a land swarming with Atheistic criminals is dropped, and we get the information that the attempt to convert people to Atheism has been a miserable failure." (20 April, 1941.)

The Prime Minister and Eden emphasised that they were still opposed to communism. Cohen saw this as "a soothing measure against certain powerful home interests, religious and other, to whom a boycott of Russia would be welcome":

> We have no great liking for Communism, but it must be met as a theory of social life and argued for and against as we discuss other social theories. Loose talk about robbery and murder, backed by lying religious opposition, will not make for the lasting peace of the world. Even Mr. Churchill may need reminding that great as are his services to the country during this war, his reputation as an authority on social and economic evolution has yet to be established; but, as we have said, we fancy that the Prime Minister's declaration was not intended for Russia at all, but for a class in this country to whom both Mussolini and Hitler owe much for the positions they now occupy. (13 July, 1941.)

An absurd feature of the establishment's dilemma over the alliance with Russia was seen in the refusal to permit the Russian national anthem to be played with that of other allies on Sunday evenings: "That is not too good an omen for the new world that is to follow the war. A desirable peace with Russia left out can be desirable only to fools — and worse. It means another armed peace which is just a degree better than actual war. But it ends in war, as experience proves." (20 July, 1941.)

The *Freethinker* did not neglect to point out that freethinkers were among the victims of Nazi persecution. Charles Bradlaugh Bonner, while appealing for funds to help freethought refugees, referred to the arrest of Captain Voska, President of the Czech Freethought Society, as soon as Hitler marched into Prague. (2 July, 1939.)

Free Speech in Wartime

Freedom of thought is hard to preserve in times of war, but the *Freethinker* stood firmly for maintaining all possible freedom of speech. In the months before war the Government promised to form a Ministry of Information if war came. Cohen immediately gave a warning: "I regard with the greatest dislike a Government propaganda that can control the news, that can suppress the truth and circulate lies whenever the Government of the day considers either of these courses advisable. If we are in earnest in fighting Fascism and other forms of tyranny, we should fight them wherever they are met." (25 June, 1939.)

Cohen feared the long-term consequences of what he called "the ministry of misinformation" and was pessimistic about the political parties' defence of independence of thought:

> Much of this we must submit to for "the duration", but we should do so with a full sense that they are restrictions, and with the resolve to end them with the war. In this last task we must not look for getting much help from the political parties. For a long time, whether we are dealing with Labour or Conservative, the tendency has been in and out of Parliament in the direction of regimentation. The party issues orders, the members of the party obey... (1 October, 1939.)

Petty British censorship was condemned. The Government at the beginning of the war decided to close cinemas, theatres and places of entertainment on Sundays. Cohen wrote: "Our soldiers showed that in the last war laughter was often escape from insanity... Bernard Shaw and Oswald Stoll have protested against the Churches being opened while the theatres are closed. Presumably the Government thinks that people do not go to Church for entertainment — unless they are Freethinkers — and that there would be no overcrowding, in any case." (17 September, 1939.) The ban on Sunday entertainment was soon modified and defenders of the Sabbath later became disturbed at the encroachment of entertainment into the Lord's Day.

The B.B.C. was, as ever, a target of the *Freethinker*'s wrath. Professor Joad's performance in the Brains Trust was especially reviled. Joad's metaphysical meanderings were seen as a betrayal by a one-time rationalist.

> Since Dr. Julian Huxley left England for the United States our irrepressible friend and philosopher, Professor C.E.M. Joad seems to have been getting quite a lot of his own way in connection with the Brains (!) Trust of the BBC.
>
> Without the personal sobering influence of Huxley's materialistic antidotes, the metaphysical toxin of Joad appears to be developing quickly of late. (22 February, 1942.)

(Huxley's refusal to call himself an atheist and enthusiasm for a non-deistic religious spirit did not always endear him to freethinkers either.)

Joad's statement at a Ministry of Information meeting that one of the troubles of to-day "was that a generation had been brought up without creed or code, and religious leaders must restore spiritual values" was sharply criticised. (22 February, 1942.) After the war a particularly strong lambasting of Joad by a Mr. Wood, coupled with a complaint about his failure to answer letters, produced a letter from Joad which began: "There now, Mr. Wood, you have drawn me!" After dealing with anti-theistic arguments and the idea that matter is not immortal Joad concluded with two questions:

> (i) Why do you always assume that when a man changes his views he does so from interested motives, or why, if you don't assume it, do you, nevertheless, contrive to imply it? (ii) Or is it only with regard to a change from views which you do hold to views which you don't, that you make this assumption and suggest this implication? Does it never occur to you that a man might *honestly* disagree with you? (4 April, 1948.)

Dorothy L. Sayers, whose radio plays about the life of Christ were very controversial because they dramatised New Testament characters using everyday language, was provoked into a very tetchy letter by Cohen's criticism of the way he saw her being used by the B.B.C. as a popular writer turned Christian apologist.

Control of information and discussion did not leave much need for use of Blasphemy Law, not yet abolished. However, "perhaps the most ridiculous blasphemy case that has ever taken place in the British Isles" was reported in 1940. A hotel proprietor in Jersey had been photographed, while lying arms outstretched and feet crossed, suntanning on the beach. A visitor gave him a copy of the photograph having used red ink to draw in nails and drops of blood in imitation of the crucifixion. The hotel proprietor put the photograph in his pocket and thought no more of it until he took it out by mistake when asked for his passport at the Aliens Office. A shocked official gave the picture to the Attorney General of the island. Proceedings went ahead and he was sentenced to one month's imprisonment. The Home Secretary refused a pardon, but cancelled what remained of the sentence as an act of clemency. The hotel proprietor's more enduring punishment was to lose his licence as a hotel keeper after being found guilty of a criminal offence.

Bombing of the Freethinker Offices

The graver events of the war threatened the *Freethinker's* continuity. Paper shortage was a continual problem and the number of pages was reduced in 1942. Bombing of cities became a serious threat in 1941. Christians, stretching apology for God's behaviour to its uttermost, suggested that London was being bombed because God wanted to give "a chance to rebuild London". The *Freethinker* poked fun at such an idea:

> When God gets to work he is too promiscuous. Someone gets hurt, but he never appears to discriminate between his friends and his enemies, although often enough, those who turn out to be his best friends are treated as his worst enemies. For all the improvements that have taken place in the character of God are due to those who were counted as opposed to him. (6 July, 1941.)

The *Freethinker* did not escape and on the evening of 10 May, 1941, its offices were burned to the ground. (The N.S.S. offices were included.) "Nothing was left but a mass of rubbish that was still smoking on May 14." The loss was severe: premises, paper, stock of books and pamphlets, and a linotype machine and other printing equipment. The most irreparable loss was between 1,000 and 1,500 volumes "representing a fine collection of (mostly) scarce books on Freethought subjects dating back to the middle eighteenth century, and some earlier of a semi-religious character."

Cohen had foreseen the danger and an emergency issue which he had kept set up ready came out on 18 May. So the continuous run of the *Freethinker* was not broken. Nor was Chapman Cohen's indefatigable spirit daunted:

> It is not well to dream plans, although we all do it. I am nearing my seventy-third birthday anniversary, and have sometimes dreamed of being able to throw on one side all the responsibilities of my position, including that of editor of the "One and Only", a post which I prize more than I should that of our Prime Minister. Not, of course, to cease writing for the paper. That is not so much work as a safety valve. But just to watch the movement in which I have spent my life growing stronger and stronger, but never so strong that it could in a state of pampered supremacy forget its history and significance and wield a slave-ship in the name of freedom.
>
> And now. Well I have, in a way, to begin all over again. To build almost from the ground upward. But German bombs can no more crush Freethought than British tyranny was able to crush or silence that band of heroic men and women who did so much to build up a heritage and to establish a tradition.
>
> The *Freethinker* goes on and with it the advanced movement. (25 May, 1941.)

As the end of the war approached, there was talk of giving thanks to the Almighty and returning to Christian values. The Bishop of Southwark said that after the war "the people must be led back to 'sanity and right values' " and that in Europe the "need for Christian literature will be enormous." The *Freethinker* was sceptical: "We have our doubts. There was no shortage of religious literature in pre-Hitler times, nor was there in any other part of Europe." (8 April, 1945.)

The Annual Report of the National Secular Society's Executive summed up the war years:

> The past six years have been a period of strain and trial, of danger and disruption such as this country has never before experienced, and in the case of a loosely knitted propagandist movement such as ours it might well have ended in complete disruption. The situation reminds one of a story that goes back to the stormy days of the French Revolution. A man, noted for his boasting, was asked what he did in the Revolution. He replied "I lived", and in sober truth that was something of an achievement. Looking back at these six years we might say with pride that we continued during one of the most trying periods of our history. Many of those who carried on the work were whisked away to some other area or joined fighting forces. Halls ceased to be available for public meetings, and travelling was reduced to a minimum. The dark streets acted as a curfew and kept people at home. These six years covered a period that we may now look back on with interest, but which we lived through with considerable discomfort. (3 June, 1945.)

Some hope was seen in an increase of membership, and a growth of financial resources, and the demand for the *Freethinker* combined with the paper shortage meant that for the only period in its history subscriptions to the *Freethinker* had to be refused. The *Freethinker* continued to circulate around the world. A consignment of freethinking books and pamphlets bound for the *Truthseeker* were seized by American custom officials: "The officials had the impudence to say that because they were anti-religious publications and in any case were not in line with the war effort, they could not be permitted to pass." (3 June, 1945.) The literature was released after legal action was taken and judgment was given in favour of the *Truthseeker*.

The 1944 Education Act

The same Annual Report drew attention to a major Parliamentary Act, which freethinkers saw as a step backwards: "Under cover of concern for a better education our war-time government succeeded in passing a Bill which restored to the Churches a great deal of the power they lost by the Education Act of 1870." (3 June, 1945.)

Freethinkers thought that the churches were taking advantage of the war to increase their influence in schools. A headline "Kidnapping" expressed this feeling and the piece stated: "If we win the war only to hand over the control of schools to the clergy we shall have paid a heavy price for victory." (8 May, 1942.) In 1941 the Archbishop of Canterbury and others had launched Five Points, which included compulsory R.I. in schools (with the right of withdrawal), R.I. as a subject for teachers' certificate, and a daily act of worship in schools. The Secular Education

League campaigned against an approach which would give greater statutory importance to religion in schools than hitherto. A leaflet was printed, signed by Professor J.B.S. Haldane, Julian Huxley, Mr. Laurence Houseman, Dr. Joseph Needham and others. It warned:

> The present international crisis, the suspension of political party controversy, and the almost complete pre-occupation of the mind of the people with the life-and-death struggle of the war have provided the opportunity long awaited by the advocates of compulsory State-aided religious education to make anew effort to secure their ends. What they could not achieve by an appeal to justice and equity they seek now to obtain through panic in a time of national emergency. (15 March, 1942.)

The extent to which the 1944 Education Act was deplored as retrogressive can be seen in a front-page article "The Education Crisis" (19 March, 1944.) A comparison was made with the vigorous campaign of Freethinkers and Nonconformist Christians so that "the State would not interpose in matters of religion" at the time of the 1870 Education Bill. "The slogan was then 'Education, Free, Compulsory and Secular'. In this 'Joe' Chamberlain was one of the leaders. In the end a compromise was agreed upon by the Churches. The Nonconformists sold the pass, and religion has been one of the strongest obstacles to a sound system of national education ever since."

In contrast, "To-day we have another clash over religious education, and this time there is an attempt by a Tory Government, which has long since outlived its legitimate span, using a majority that dare not face the electorate with the religious clauses of the Bill now before the House of Commons."

Talk about "religious equality" by the Minister of Education was described as "humbug, for when our Prime Minister and the Minister of Education talk about religious equality they mean at most equality among the Christians." There was no hope that

> Atheists would be permitted to enter the State schools in order to teach pupils what science has to say concerning the origin of gods — all the gods. The utmost favour bestowed upon these would be the withdrawal of children from religious instruction which the parents disliked. But the saturation of the whole of the school time is aimed at; and it takes a politician to appreciate the favour of not being compelled to eat a dinner one doesn't like, but to be still forced to pay for one that he will not eat. Christian freedom is a very curious thing whenever and wherever it is encountered. (19 March, 1944.)

Another front-page on education expressed opposition to R.I. on the basic grounds that it was not true education, with knowledge being imparted and a sense of inquiry encouraged:

> The "great lying creed" as Heine called it, is dying. That is why the clergy feel that by some method the children must be captured. With all other subjects the teacher can afford to wait until his pupil is able to appreciate the quality of what is being told him; with religion, belief must precede conviction. The pupils of the parsonage cannot wait until development is expressed in understanding. (14 May, 1944.)

The Butler Education Act was passed and justified freethinkers' fears that it would give religion a firm footing in schools in subsequent decades. In contrast to the continued strength of worship and religious education in schools there has been a general gain in scepticism which has come from wider education in the post-war years.

The End of War

The end of war saw the *Freethinker* commenting upon the forthcoming celebrations, deploring the bloodshed and lamenting the trumpeted thanksgivings:

> We are writing these notes while everyone is anxiously awaiting the news that Germany has surrendered. Every arrangement has been made to "celebrate": the public-houses are to have a larger quantity of beer and the Prime Minister has asked all the churches to open their doors and return thanks to God for our "victory". We fancy that this piece of advice is given with an eye on the coming General Election rather than an expression of Mr. Churchill's profound religious feeling. But votes are votes, and to get the religious vote on the side of A or B or C is very important for political success. After all, votes are votes, and two of them will overcome one without the slightest regard to their ethical or social value. Certain it is, from the wider point of view, that religion has been one of the casualties of the war. No war has started with a greater outburst of "the trumpets of the Lord", and never was the futility of the trumpeting made more obvious. To the common man it would seem that God should have done his best to prevent the war, or if the war escaped his notice, some very plain exhibition of his interference — on our side, of course — should have occurred. A deity who stands looking on while the terrible brutality of the German Nazis manifested itself seems to fall short of what sense and decency would expect. Still, the combination of more beer and an outbreak of thanks to God for giving us victory may go well together. There are many forms of intoxication, and a combination of all forms is a very powerful thing. Still, there seems to be something wrong in a deity who stands, or sits, idly by watching the terrors of the German prisons and then receiving thanks from his children for ending the war after five years of bloodshed, brutality and disaster. Returning thanks to God in the present situation merely emphasises that both camels and Christians take their burdens kneeling. (13 May, 1945.)

Further bloodshed and brutality were to cap the horrors of the war in Europe and point to a major factor in the second half of the twentieth century: the dropping of atomic bombs at Hiroshima and Nagasaki. Cohen foresaw a new scale of horror for war and urged the need for international control:

> The sanction given to the use of atomic bombs has stripped war of all its "glories", and marks miscellaneous killing as perfectly proper. The world war has shown armed conflict at its greatest and at its worst. But you cannot marry the higher social qualities by wiping out old and young, good and bad, with complete immunity. To-day, we now call the dropping of atomic bombs war; we are afraid history will give it an uglier name.

...I think there is one way out, and only one. I have been pressing for it for about fifty years without much apparent success. I suggest that each of the "civilised" countries — the uncivilised are not really dangerous — should agree to complete national disarmament and leave the settlement of any disputes that may arise to an international court, which alone should wield sufficient material forces to enforce their decisions. But the courts must have adequate power to enforce their verdicts. The courts now existing have no such power. If one of the disputants refuses to obey the court the case drops. So long as the methods that now obtain are in force, chaos and war will continue, and so long shall we be threatened with wars, or what is almost as bad, perpetual preparation for war. (19 August, 1945.)

Post-War Concerns

Features of the post-war period which are represented in the pages of the *Freethinker* include the new Attlee Government, the relationship between Europe and the communist countries, McCarthyism and threats to freedom of speech, the resurgence of independence movements in the colonies, and a discussion of social reform in areas of private morality. Christianity had lost further ground and secularism had to find a new role in a broadly secular society.

In December 1943 the Archbishops of Canterbury and York had appointed a commission to find out why Christianity was losing ground. When the Report was issued, the *Freethinker* quoted the Report's admission that "The loss of ground was very real": "There can be no doubt that there is a wide and deep gulf between the Church and the people... The evidence, therefore, of chaplains and others in close touch with all three Services, and with munition factories, may be accepted as conclusive. They testify with one voice to the fact of a wholesale drift from organised religion." (9 December, 1945.)

The long-term drift was seen in a wide-ranging social survey, the Rowntree Report on "English Life and Leisure", published in 1951. Between 1901 and 1948 the proportion of the adult population who attended any church service in one area fell from 35.5 per cent to 13 per cent. Anglicanism suffered disproportionately, and during the same period the percentage of church attendances made by Roman Catholics rose from 13.8 to 31.1 per cent. The *Freethinker* drew the conclusion that the Established Church was an anomaly: "These figures, we submit, constitute an irresistible argument for the immediate Disestablishment and Disendowment of the Established Church, not only upon secularist but upon the most elementary democratic principles." (8 July, 1951.)

The *Freethinker* contained surprisingly little about the Attlee Government, but that was due to the journal's claims to be non-political and the divisiveness of socialism among secularists. Can an article by C. McCall, "A Plea for Individualism", be seen as an oblique comment on the effects of a Labour Government:

Freethought and individualism are inseparable... Not that the Freethinker

> disregards the welfare of the community, this is far from the case. He realises that man can only achieve true happiness by co-operation in communal life, but this is very different from submerging the individual in the mass... We live, of course, in a world which is more "communised" or more "collectivised" than ever before, due to the influence of machine development... The progressive course, I maintain, can only be pursued with a scientific, freethinking, individualistic attitude of mind. (16 September, 1945.)

An article on "The New Morality" by R.A. Rasmussen included comment upon socialism:

> Socialism, which has engendered such wide works in opposition to some of life's greatest inequalities, revolves largely on the principle of private enterprise being immoral... Among modern states the general trend is for the State to take over the larger monopolies, usually those serving the people's basic requirements, while controlling lesser economic units and urging them towards public service. The spirit appears to be that it does not matter about the fundamental ethic of private enterprise if it can be made to serve the community. (7 October, 1945.)

The most re-iterated comment about the Attlee Government was a complaint about the influence of Sir Stafford Cripps "where the economics of austerity require to be buttressed by Theology and where the only surplus commodity is the Bread from Heaven." (Ridley — 15 January, 1950.) Cripps, entrusted with responsibility to get us out of "the financial and industrial mess in which the late war has landed us" was castigated for associating himself with a Universal Week of Prayer: "He has already exhorted us to tighten our belts, to work harder, to save, to avoid wasted effort and to help the export trade, so we may be excused for inquiring whether by leading a 'prayer drive' he is himself using his energies for the country's good." (25 January, 1948.)

The General Election of 1951 produced the comment: "A General Election has, as such, little to do with *Free* thought or, indeed, perhaps with thought of any kind." (14 October, 1951.) Nevertheless, secularists were urged to raise with candidates matters such as Blasphemy Law, the State Church and the BBC's use of religion. There was some regret that the association of anti-religious criticism with "advanced radical criticism of the social order" had declined, leading to "a one-sided view of secularism... confined purely and simply to anti-theological criticism.":

> This is the more surprising in the mid-twentieth century when our enemies, the churches, are all working overtime as political "pressure groups"...
>
> ... The final goal of secular society can, however, only be realised by pursuing and enlarging the goal of democracy which implies that secularist politics consist in supporting everything which tends towards the ultimate goal of a secular society and in opposing everything which hinders its attainment, a conception of politics which, we repeat, will be found frequently to cut right across party alignments. (28 October, 1951.)

The democratic commitment was firm, and the attitude to marxism and communist countries was keenly debated — especially in the correspondence columns. A typical comment from a prolonged exchange came in a letter from John Rowland, headed "Marxism Once More", which responded to the views of Archibald Robertson:

> I hold that for anyone to be free in his thought, it is extremely dangerous to hand over one's reason to an authoritarian body. I hold that this is equally true of the R.C. Church and of any and every political party. Mr. Robertson may complain that this tends to play into the hands of the war-mongers; but the Communist and Tory seem to me to be the people who play into the hands of the war-mongers, as the present situation in Berlin shows, since Mr. Bevin is, in his foreign policy, indistinguishable from a Tory, and Mr. Molotov is certainly a Communist. (19 September, 1948.)

Affairs in Eastern Europe were followed with interest in the *Freethinker*. For example, the trial of the Primate Cardinal Mindszenty in Hungary, which created a sense of outrage among Catholics, provoked the headline "Pot Calling the Kettle Black" for an article by F.A. Ridley, which claimed that the Cardinal's trial was a result of the political action of the Catholic Church, not a persecution of belief. (27 February, 1949.) However, another article by Francis L. Gould called Ridley's view of the trial "a model of shortsightedness masquerading as rationalism", and said "Nothing justifies, nothing can ever justify, injustice. The trial is taking place for the sole purpose of getting rid of a political opponent." (27 February, 1949.)

Similar arguments took place about life in Russia. It was agreed that the British press could not be giving an unbiased picture of the socialist-atheist state. A factual account of the Russian economy included a mild criticism of Stalin: "All departure from academic orthodoxy, save in one instance when Stalin repudiated a quaint theory of the origin of language, is frowned upon." (28 October, 1951.) A frequent *Freethinker* correspondent, who had spent five years in Russia, wrote enthusiastically of the "tremendous vitality of the Soviet civilisation" (27 July, 1952), but this was countered by a reference to Shostakovich and Akhmatova and the "muzzling of free and individual expression."

There was quite an argument about the extent to which the National Secular Society was influenced by communism. After the Annual Demonstration in 1951, a letter complained of a "torrent of Communist propaganda" (8 July, 1951), but subsequent accounts appear to suggest no more than some criticism of America, dissatisfaction with "Wall Street Capitalism" and a minor reproach for the frivolity of the members of the public sporting themselves at the Festival of Britain South Bank Illuminations.

Freethinkers could not be expected to have any time for a "Red Scare" or McCarthyite witch hunting. In an article entitled "The Roots of British Hypocrisy" Tom Hill saw the "Red Scare" as a modern version of heaven and hell:

> When God leaves us the Red Devil must be invented in his stead.
>
> You have, of course, heard of the big "cop" who said to the little man: "Scram, you red-hot Communist" and when the little man protested that he was an anti-communist, the "cop" shouted: "I don't care a damn what sort of Communist you are — scram!"
>
> The fear of death and damnation had worked for thousands of years to protect rulers in power. It does not work in this "enlightened" century of ours, but millions of people are easily taken in with the "Red Scare", the modern version of heaven and hell. (19 September, 1948.)

The same author pointed to a nexus between American business, Moral Rearmament, and the pursuit of communism and godlessness:

> Paul Hoffman — the automobile magnate who is the Marshall plan administrator — sent the Moral Rearmament Assembly a message declaring that it was "giving the world the ideological counterpart of the Marshall plan". Thus, along with dried eggs, the U.S. means, under the Marshall plan, to export "superior ideas". Under cover of "soul-saving", religious hysteria and appeals for class collaboration, N.A.M. (National Association of Manufacturers) wants to use the Buchmanites as an additional instrument for spreading its propaganda for organising espionage and details of "Marshall Aid". Their "ideological weapons" will turn out to be very material weapons for world-wide exploitation. (22 April, 1948.)

Later an article on McCarthyism by Leon Spain described it as "an intellectual and social excrescence". The article lists some religious groups involved:

> Among the agencies and organisations who determine what views are acceptable and unacceptable are such censorious bodies as the American Legion, the Veterans of Foreign Wars, Daughters of the American Revolution, the Roman Catholic Hierarchy, and other bodies who regard with the gravest suspicion anyone who openly ventures to question their professed principles, which they deem unchallengeable and beyond criticism... A movement is well under way to revise historical textbooks in accordance with their views, and the pressure from the aforesaid guardians of legitimate expression, has been to describe "godlessness" as one of the cardinal evils of American life... (15 January, 1954.)

The *Freethinker*, always an opponent of racial injustice, saw the justice of self-government for former colonies and protectorates. British rule in India had never been idealised by the *Freethinker* and the attempt "to settle affairs in India" was welcomed in 1942:

> But the move would have come with greater grace if it had been done earlier in a generous spirit, and if the old school tie brigade and the army of "get money, honestly if you can, but get it", could have divested themselves of the belief that India's main purpose on the earth was to provide openings for our trade, posts for a certain number of men who believe they have a legitimate claim for good posts and comfortable pensions. (29 March, 1942.)

Looking back on the violence between Hindus and Muslims in the Punjab at the time of the creation of an independent India and Pakistan (as a Muslim state), G.B. Singh, an Indian freethinker retired in

England, deplored the religious aspect of the massacres:

> ...the people who were engaged in this mutual slaughter, and in acts worse than slaughter, did not represent any political parties, but three religious communities. All that has happened was done in the name of religion, for its glory, and for the greater glory of God, who they claim, has inspired their religions. Each one of them claims that his religion teaches him the Fatherhood of God, and the Brotherhood of man, and that it teaches him to love others, and not to take revenge for the injuries received. And yet, the events give the lie direct to these claims. (22 April, 1948.)

The position of colonial Africa was seen as blighted by missionaries: "An African publicist has recently reminded us that in his native land first came the missionary cadres with the Bible and Cross, followed by the traders with gin and Lancashire cotton goods, and finally, the plume-helmeted pro-Consuls, backed by the armed forces of the annexing power." (26 March, 1950.)

There was a report of a meeting at which Alan Paton, author of *Cry The Beloved Country,* spoke on the relationship between blacks and whites in South Africa and "blurted out" how the "missionary endeavour has been characterised by a blundering entry into a delicate province..." (19 March, 1950.)

An article in which Paul Robeson asked "What Now for the Negro?" was reprinted from the *Modern Thinker.* Freethinkers would certainly have endorsed his views:

> ...in all countries negroes must stand in one camp, fighting for freedom and social justice. We have not the slightest idea of Africa, as a united continent of negroes, ever standing against the other races. No, all our hope lies in the development of freedom in the world. But meanwhile negroes should unite and systematically develop their own culture. The world today is full of barbarism, and I feel that this united negro culture could bring into the world a fresh spiritual, humanitarian principle, a principle of human friendship and service to the community. (30 August, 1942.)

The "New Morality" was an old phrase for the title of an article outlining important developments in areas of concern to secularists:

> The stigma which the old morality had woven around sex is being steadily removed. In despair the traditionalist peppers mankind with warnings of the debasement of all human values, of the wild abandonment of man and the final holocaust to which he is approaching. The humanist is unmoved by such appeals. (7 October, 1945.)

Birth control, marriage and women's rights had been much discussed, but hitherto homosexuality had been given rather scant attention. *(The Well of Loneliness* was discussed mainly as a free speech issue, see p. 64). An absence of comment on the Wilde case at the end of the previous century was remedied by C.G.L. Du Cann's enthusiastic review of *Oscar Wilde: A Summing Up* by Lord Alfred Douglas. Du Cann praised Wilde for being, despite his nominal Catholicism, a freethinker "in the best sense of the word": "He could and did think new thoughts. His mind was free as Ariel's." Lord Queensberry, the outspoken freethinker who had helped to bring about Wilde's downfall, was condemned: "It is not given to many men to ruin a genius: Lord Queensberry ruined two." Du Cann also thought homosexuality should not be treated as a crime: "In fact homosexuality is still a challenge today when sensible folk and many judges regard some of its manifestations as illness of body or mind fitter for the doctor or psychologist than the prison warder or as a private vice rather than a public crime." (10 March, 1940.)

Reminiscences of Queensberry and Douglas from a freethinking correspondent, Edgar Syers, led to an interesting correspondence in which Alfred Douglas participated. (March, April, 1940.) Edgar Syers and Alfred Douglas argued about their memories of whether Queensberry had planned to thrash Wilde. Douglas wrote: "As to my father's threats to thrash Wilde, it is not disputed that he made them, but I have already pointed out in my book and in your columns that they were nothing but crazy vapourings treated by Wilde with contempt..." (12 May, 1940.)

George Bedborough, who played so questionable a role in the fracas surrounding the publication of *Sexual Inversion* by Havelock Ellis became an intermittent *Freethinker* contributor in the twenties and thirties. He wrote about Ellis on his death in 1939, regarding him as "essentially secularist in outlook". He praised his scientific study of sexuality: "The fact that *Sexual Inversion* was most repellent to unscientific readers — especially the pious and puritanical — did not weigh with this courageous writer." (23 July, 1939.)

A direct plea for a change in the law came in an article "Homosexuality — Morals and the Law" by C.H. Norman. (8 January, 1954). He thought Royal Commissions were an ineffective means of dealing with injustice: "Therefore, the suggestion of a Royal Commission or a Departmental Committee (which authorities would probably prefer) is hardly sufficient to deal with a situation in which numbers of persons are being heavily punished for conduct which many parts of the world regard not only as properly outside the province of the criminal law, but as a matter for mental or psychological treatment in proper institutions." While talk of "treatment" is anathema to homosexuals today, who regard their sexual orientation as a legitimate variation, it was an advance in the forties and fifties to move away from persecution and criminalisation.

Secularists saw prison as a means of rehabilitation or safeguarding the community from danger, not as a form of vengeance. The *Freethinker*, therefore, contained vigorous opposition to hanging. An article "Hanging and the Christian Way of Life" referred to an unsuccessful attempt to bring in a Bill to eliminate hanging, flogging and other brutal punishments. Opposition in the Lords came from the Bishops of Canterbury and Truro, and the remarks of the Prelate of Winchester were reported; he feared the "effect of abolishing the death penalty on the education of the conscience of the community." People might, he suspected, "lose their general sense of the wickedness of wickedness" —

a phrase about which the *Freethinker* remarked "that is obscure, but sounds nasty". (22 April, 1948.)

Another moral issue leading to a call for legal reform was voluntary euthanasia. A vigorous plea, "Let's Legalise Voluntary Euthanasia", came in an article by Robert H. Scott from the U.S.A.:

> Let us therefore, my fellow citizens, without needless delay, take appropriate action through our legislature to legalise, with adequate safeguards against fraud and abuse, voluntary medical euthanasia for incurably suffering adults of sound mind and, upon the court-approved petition of relatives or legal guardians, for irremediably suffering babes, children, and adolescents, and also older persons who, for one reason or another, are mentally incompetent. Let us unlock with the key of humanitarian good sense and let us remove the anti-euthanasia handcuffs that well-meaning but misguided custodians of certain religious beliefs and fears have fastened upon the wrists of the physician...
>
> Remember, my fellow citizens, *some day it will be your turn to die.* (21 May, 1950.)

The End of Cohen's Leadership

Such social issues were to become an increasingly important aspect of secularism. At a time when anti-theological arguments meant little to a society whose knowledge of the Bible and Christian dogma was vanishing, and when failure to resolve an individualist or socialist position towards economics prevented a direct political involvement, the National Secular Society and the *Freethinker* were seeking a new role. The word "Humanism" was gaining currency for a less bible-bashing, more ethically centred version of secularism. Cohen was not enthusiastic about the word when three talks on "Humanism" took place on the B.B.C. by Professor Sir Julian Huxley, Dr. Gilbert Murray and Mr. Oldham (the Editor of the *Christian Newsletter*).

Cohen thought the talks baulked the "real issue" of theism versus atheism, and queried the word "humanist":

> But the term "humanist". One wonders what it meant in the mind of Professor Huxley and Mr. Oldham. If used in its historical sense, it is a term that belongs to a past phase of European history. It was, some centuries ago, a term that characterised a revolt against the Catholic Church and indicated a belief that man might shape his own destiny by his own effort and understanding. There is also "humanism" which is a name for a philosophic outlook such as was held by William James in America, and by his follower or co-worker in England, Mr. F.C.S. Schiller. Substantially, that philosophy might be expressed by a term that carries us right back to the ancient Greeks: "Man is the measure of all things". A vital truth even if it is not the answer to all problems. And humanism in the sense of acting wisely and kindly to one's fellows is, in however distorted a sense, common to the human race, and beyond that to the higher animal world. Man is, after all, a social animal, and his feelings, ideas and actions must have some reference to his fellow humans. To some extent every human being is a "humanist"; and when Huxley called

> himself a "scientific humanist" and Oldham decided that he was a "Christian humanist", in the eyes of many both might have written themselves down as "humorists", even though belonging to the unconscious variety. What really divided these two was a belief in God: not in the nature of God, but in his existence. And for purposes of clarity the issue would have been stated as "Atheism versus Theism". But that would never have been permitted on a B.B.C. platform, which practises our Prime Minister's plan, "What we have we hold". But we see no objection to the term "humanist" being applied to everybody from dustman to duke and from fool to philosopher. (23 January, 1944.)

Cohen was moving towards the end of a magnificent innings as editor of the *Freethinker* and President of the National Secular Society. Some of his writing became repetitive in later years, and the *Freethinker* did not escape some arid debates and tedious reworking of arguments against Christianity. Debates about whether James Joyce was a genius or a charlatan, whether Shakespeare had written Shakespeare, and whether psychoanalysis is an illusion were not of a high level. Even arguments about the historicity of Jesus brought little evidence that had not been marshalled in the days of Foote and Bradlaugh. Herbert Cutner, a longstanding and valued contributor, who participated in some of these quarrels, was warned by a correspondent to "avoid forming a habit of quibbling and wanton disputation." *Freethinker* contributors always needed such a reminder, but it was especially appropriate to the latter years of Cohen's reign.

A few days before his 85th birthday Joseph McCabe, another venerable freethinker who had been associated mainly with the Rationalist Press Association, gave a lecture entitled "Religion, Crime and Secularism" at the invitation of the West London Branch of the National Secular Society. But the era of these great rationalists, bridging the nineteenth and twentieth centuries with astonishing vigour and longevity, was almost over.

In 1949 Cohen resigned as President of the N.S.S., a position he had held since 1915. Mr. R.H. Rosetti, who had been General Secretary since 1927, was made acting President, a position confirmed by election at the Annual General Meeting in the following year. As reported in the *Freethinker*, it was a surprisingly low-key transfer of power, maybe because Cohen remained editor of the *Freethinker*. A tribute from the Executive Council was printed: "Under his able guidance, Freethought propaganda began to take on a more scientific and philosophic turn from which it has never turned back. His ability and the confidence he inspired soon began to bear fruit in another direction. Sympathisers in the movement felt safe in leaving money to the Society, and to-day, the National Secular Society can spend on its propaganda more than ever before in its history." (26 June, 1949.)

During the next two years his editorship of the *Freethinker* was evidently less active, and he no longer wrote the front page article with such regularity. F.A. Ridley and, to a lesser extent, H. Cutner, were writing front-page pieces. In 1951, at the age of 83, presumably with great reluctance, he resigned as editor. He wrote:

> My sixty years of active service have been packed with the common experience of leaders in a great but unpopular cause: there have been ups and downs, sunshine and storms, rejoicings and disappointments, but never for a moment have I regretted having given of my best to Freethought during those sixty years. I have made many very dear friends and colleagues during my work in the movement and although I must now return my sword to its scabbard, I hold a rich store of happy memories in the grand fight with the army of human liberation against ignorance, superstition, and priestcraft. (27 May, 1951.)

There were many tributes to Cohen's work. His successor as editor, F.A. Ridley, wrote that he was "conscious of shouldering a heavy task": "To expect to emulate either the brilliant style, coruscating wit, or remarkable literary flair of G.W. Foote, or the profound philosophical grasp, keen analytical insight, and unsurpassed lucidity of Chapman Cohen, would be a well nigh impossible ambition." (17 June, 1951.)

Cohen's last few years were sad for a man to whom mental exploration, reading, and writing and discussion had been the essence of life. At his cremation on 11 February, 1954, an address by P. Victor Morris referred to Mrs. Cohen's support "while loss of memory, speech and sight gradually robbed him of everything he valued apart from her comradeship and care." In writing of the death and old age of others, he always stressed the inevitability of the course of nature, rather than sorrow or tragedy, and thus he would have wished others to react to his own end.

His death at the age of 85 on 4 February, 1954, was marked by numerous tributes to his achievements. Pages of appreciative comments appear in several issues of the *Freethinker,* referring to his platform gifts, his great leadership, and "Dear old C.C.! " C. Bradlaugh Bonner wrote that his death "marks a milestone in the story of British Freethought".

F.A. Ridley, who had succeeded R.H. Rosetti as President of the National Secular Society on his untimely death in 1951, wrote a front-page *Freethinker* article entitled "The Passing of a Great Man": "With the passing of Mr. Chapman Cohen, a great age passes as well; we now approach the end of that 'century of stupendous progress' from the Freethought angle which began with Charles Bradlaugh and ended with Chapman Cohen." Ridley surveyed what he saw as "Three sequential phases" of the "historic Freethought Movement, which began with Owen, Holyoake and Bradlaugh." The first was a phase of "political Secularism" under the leadership of Charles Bradlaugh, when the "British Secular Movement was concerned primarily with its legal recognition, with its elemental right to exist at all as a *legal* body, with the right to free speech on Freethought platforms and on anti-religious topics, in face of both the outrageous Blasphemy Laws and the 'moral' — and, at times, physical — pressure exerted by the Church". The second stage Ridley saw as the era of "bible banging" which was led by G.W.

Foote, "and in the era of which we are speaking, this mode of attack was absolutely necessary and, indeed was rendered absolutely inevitable by the crude bibliolatry which, as the present writer can testify from personal experience in his own youth, was then rampant and virtually universal in religious circles..." The third phase was characterised by the intellectual approach of Chapman Cohen. "Mr. Cohen emphasised — and with what lucidity! — the *positive* philosophy of Atheism... it is, perhaps, by his philosophical analysis of Materialism rather than by his more controversial writings that the second Editor of *The Freethinker* is, we think, most likely to be remembered." (19 February, 1954.)

In *A Sort of Autobiography* Cohen wrote of himself:

> The compliment I have most valued was that paid me by a Labour leader who, at a public meeting, had the courage to thank one of the best-known Atheists in Britain for the help he had given others to look at life.
>
> If ever any friend is interested enough to write an epitaph over my grave, the one I think I would value most is: "He took the best from others and gave his best to the world."

CHAPTER VI
CAMPAIGNING AND COMBATING SUPERSTITION

The last quarter of the *Freethinker's* history has witnessed considerable changes in format, content and editorship. There are continuous themes such as the remaining power of the churches, a desire for social change, and a moral concern and distaste for all forms of cant. New issues and emphases emerge as the *Freethinker* responds to the "new theology", the growth of cults and superstition, comparative religion, and the challenge of emotional, anti-intellectual, anti-science currents. A less stable editorship and problems of inflation led to many more changes in style and layout than in the previous seventy-five years.

F.A. Ridley was editor from 1951 to 1954, for a while, like Cohen, combining this with the role of President of the National Secular Society. His regular contributions began in the 1940s and he remained a contributor until the early 1970s. He was born in 1897 and, displaying the vigorous longevity of some freethinkers, he gave what he claimed would be his last public lecture during the centenary year of the *Freethinker*. Unlike Foote and Cohen, he was an enthusiastic socialist with an allegiance to the Independent Labour Party and was as prolific a contributor to the *Socialist Leader* as to the *Freethinker*. On many occasions he must have almost simultaneously written front-page articles for both journals.

Ridley was an established writer by the time he became editor of the *Freethinker*, having published books such as *The Papacy and Fascism* (1937), *The Evolution of the Papacy* (published by the Pioneer Press, an imprint of G.W. Foote & Co.), and *Revolutionary Tradition in England*. He was political and scholarly, having been expelled from the Trotskyites by Trotsky himself, and being a familiar figure in the British Museum Reading Room. His short period as editor and President was due to his temperamental preference for writing and research to administration and organisation.

Ridley brought to his *Freethinker* writing a belief that the Roman Catholic Church was the most powerful enemy of progress and reason, and that freethought should not lose sight of its essentially radical tradition. He also brought a global perspective, writing about Islam, Eastern Europe and Africa. (He was a personal friend of Jomo Kenyatta.)

In an article headed "Freethought Faces the Future" he asked "What are the contemporary drifts of civilisation to-day, and how do they affect the contemporary movement for intellectual and social emancipation which is comprised under the heading of Secularism?" After writing of the "drift towards an atomic holocaust", he turned to the Roman Catholic Church:

> At the Vatican, they take long views. One must not confound temporary tactics of accommodation with their long term fundamental strategy. Beyond all its manoeuvres dictated by circumstances of an age of rapid

> change, the papacy pursues a single and constant aim with a single-minded and ruthless zeal: the destruction of modern secular civilisation and the re-introduction of medieval ways of life. In the new Dark Age, in which science would have committed suicide, Rome would once again reign as of old over a medieval theocracy, and heretics and Atheists would have but the choice, which was theirs for a thousand years, to obey or die. (1 January, 1950.)

Around the world Ridley saw an alliance of "spiritual" and secular reaction, in the regime of Franco in Spain, and in "the Islamic theocracy of Pakistan, in Calvinistic South Africa, in the newly-formed State of Israel, the identical phenomenon is visible: the reaction in Church and State."

In asking whether religion has a future he took a long-term view:

> ...since the industrial revolution, human society has been sent hurtling forward under the ceaseless dynamic impact of a non-stop permanent revolution in its technical foundations... it seems to be a reasonable assumption that an indefinite prolongation of the current technically based civilization must, sooner or later, but in any case inevitably, bring about the final collapse of the supernaturalistic and animistic pre-scientific ideas which form the fundamental core of all religions. Or put more briefly, that an industrial civilization must ultimately destroy religion. Such an assumption is, indeed, assumed by the most profound and influential modern social thinkers, however much they may diverge in other respects; it is, for example, common to such modern masters as Auguste Comte, St. Simon, Herbert Spencer, and Karl Marx. (Ibid.)

His intellectual perspective is much more European and socialist than that of most *Freethinker* contributors.

His allegiance to secularism, as he saw it, was firm:

> ...the philosophy of Secularism is, to-day, actually more necessary than ever before... Since the social crisis of our times is incomparably more urgent than was the case two generations ago when The *Freethinker* was first launched in a Victorian world which, despite the then current power of religious bigotry and the stormy, controversial arena in which the paper's founders waged their bitter struggle for intellectual existence, yet possessed a social optimism and a confident anticipation of progress which our age seems largely to have lost. We may, perhaps, express the difference in an adequate sentence, if we remark that, whereas to that generation science implied progress, to our generation it instinctively suggests atomic war and conjures up the resulting spectre of universal social dissolution... (Ibid.)

An apocalyptic feel to some of Ridley's writing and almost a "world conspiracy" view of the Vatican make him uncharacteristic of the mainstream freethought tradition of Foote and Cohen, but he widened the *Freethinker's* perspective and raised the temperature of controversies which had lain dormant in the latter years of Cohen's reign.

Following Ridley's resignation in 1954 an Editorial Committee consisting of G.H. Taylor, F.A. Hornibrook and Bayard Simmons took editorial responsibility. G.H. Taylor was interested in science and the history of the freethought movement and compiled *A Chronology of British Secularism* (N.S.S. 1957). F.A. Hornibrook was a genial and longstanding secularist, also famous as a physiotherapist who had written the popular book *The Culture of the Abdomen* (1924). Bayard Simmons had been the first "suffra gent" imprisoned for female suffrage (1906) and contributed occasional poems to the *Freethinker* for many years.

In 1957 Colin McCall joined the Editorial Board and Bayard Simmons retired from it. McCall was active among Northern branches of the National Secular Society and had contributed reports and articles to the *Freethinker.* He was General Secretary of the Society from 1955 until 1963. McCall became the most active member of the Editorial Board and in due course became the sole editor. The range of his own writing is wide — from philosophy to theatre. In 1965 he wrote: "Pressure of other work has necessitated my resignation from a job that I have been proud to hold for nearly a decade." His successful editorial policy had been "to keep the *Freethinker* independent and non-sectarian; to encourage — though not uncritically — all branches of the secular-humanist movement; to give expression to varied and opposing points of view when they seemed worth considering and were reasonably stated." (31 December, 1965.)

A period of very rapid turnover ensued. David Tribe, who was so forthright and active a President of the National Secular Society, held the fort for seven months (January to July 1966), writing: "When I took the job last January it was entirely, like Pope John's pontificate, as a 'stop-gap'. I trust that I too have passed on without stirring things up too much..." (27 May, 1966.) Seven months were long enough to give the paper a more modern appearance and to give prominence to major international events. He wrote that "most welcomed the inclusion of current political comment though they did not necessarily agree with particular comments" and made no apology for "blunt words on Rhodesia and Vietnam".

Kit Mouat succeeded David Tribe for five months (August 1966 to January 1967). She was a former artist and a poet, and the founder of the international Humanist Letter Network. She introduced personal articles from readers describing "How I Became a Humanist" and invited much discussion of the role of humanism.

David Collis was editor from January to November in 1967. His front pages were very idiosyncratic and included free verse on public events, dialogues, open letters, personal reminiscences and headlines such as "Ban Sex It's Too Enjoyable".

From November 1967 to August 1968 Karl Hyde was editor. He aimed for shorter articles and encouraged discussions of humanism and militant freethought which seem somewhat insubstantial in retrospect. In a note on "Another Change of Editor for the Freethinker" (5 July, 1968), at the time of his resignation, evidence of tension between Hyde and the Board of G.W. Foote broke out. Indeed, Karl Hyde in one of his remaining issues was sufficiently ill-humoured to write, in a front page about a meeting to commemorate the centenary of Cohen's birth, — "Frankly, I attended this meeting only through a sense of duty and in anticipation of impending boredom." (19 July, 1968.)

The instability of editorship may be partly attributed to the difficulty of paying a reasonable salary for a full-time job. (It cannot be over-emphasised how much of the work which has sustained the *Freethinker* has been done with no or minimal remuneration.) However, personal quarrels and tensions, naturally not recorded in the *Freethinker* pages, can be assumed to have played a part in the rapid editorial changes. Nor is it an accident that these years saw vigorous growth of secularist and humanist activity, for such periods are likely to create conflict between old and new outlooks and throw up less committed individuals.

David Reynolds, who was editor from September 1968 to July 1970, was the youngest editor, being under the legal majority of 21 at the time when he started and leaving to take up a university place. He persuaded new writers to contribute, and introduced photographs, interviews and a regular cartoon by Daly. He continued Tribe's determination to keep the *Freethinker* squarely in touch with the crises of the modern world. A typically wide-ranging front-page was headed "A Holy Mess" and began: "Egypt and Israel, India and Pakistan, Federal Nigeria and the breakaway 'Biafra', are the prime examples at the present time of strife stemming from deep-seated religious differences" and went on to discuss the situation in Northern Ireland. (19 October, 1968.)

William McIlroy migrated from his position as General Secretary to that of editor in 1970. His journalistic flair and sense of humour are well-known to current readers. Within a few months, he was running stories like the one headed "Nun-Running Scandal Hits the Vatican" about a nun-running racket from the poverty-stricken Indian state of Kerala to meet a shortage of Catholic nuns. His exposure of the indoctrination tactics of sects and cults was ahead of its time. As a former General Secretary of the National Secular Society he was in a good position to use the *Freethinker* as a campaigning arm and he did much to gain media publicity for secularist activities. He edited the journal from 1970 to 1971, throughout 1975 and 1976, and returned in 1981.

Nigel Sinnott edited the journal for one and a half years from the beginning of 1972. He had a specialist interest in freethought history and his own line drawings and cartoons brought charm as well as bite to the *Freethinker*. His very individual sense of humour was displayed when he wrote his "Nunc Dimittis": "And now my time has come to depart: to hang up my sledgehammer, collect my silk hat and frock coat, and bid you good wishes and success for the future. By your leave, *il faut cultiver notre aspidistra.*" (September, 1973.) During his editorship in 1973 the *Freethinker* was forced, for financial reasons to become monthly instead of weekly with 16 rather than 8 pages. This has ensured its survival, but was clearly a loss, especially in the possibility of news topicality.

Christopher Morey, whose editorship ran from November 1973 to December 1974, worked under the enormous pressure of a simultaneous demanding full-time job. His editorship is marked by an emphasis on politics and current affairs.

Jim Herrick edited the *Freethinker* from January 1977 to June 1981, after having been assistant editor to W. McIlroy for one year.

During the last 20 years the *Freethinker* has moved office three times. In 1959 there was a move from 41 Gray's Inn Road to 103 Borough High Street, and a move in 1973 to 698 Holloway Road was soon followed by a shift to 702 Holloway Road. A change of printer became essential when a pious compositor censored, sabotaged, and then refused to set entire sections of the paper in 1974.

William Griffiths, Treasurer of G.W. Foote & Co. and the National Secular Society, must be mentioned as an individual whose determination, hard work and shrewdness were outstanding. Without his behind-the-scene efforts the *Freethinker* could not have survived. Nor should the numerous unnamed sellers and distributors be forgotten. They did not allow the risks of unpopularity and (in the early days) prosecution to deter their enthusiastic support of freethought.

One outstandingly regular contributor to the *Freethinker* was Herbert Cutner (1881-1969) who wrote regular articles from the 1920s to the 1960s. He produced much of the Acid Drops and, later, This Believing World columns and he was assistant to Cohen. He was an artist and controversialist with somewhat right-wing views. He was widely known as an investigator and debunker of spiritualism. On 10 July 1959 he published "In Retrospect", his 1,000th article:

> Religion in general and Christianity in particular were receiving some very hard knocks from Freethought in those so different days before World War I... The two wars and the rise of the radio and TV have in no small measure changed all that. The Churches have captured the latter, and so are able to put across a world-wide publicity at no cost to themselves which, if we think soberly about it, is staggering. And the worst thing about it is that even if they have not convinced many people, it is because they have become merely apathetic. They do not want, if they can help it, even to think... (10 July, 1959.)

Critics of Christianity

Knocking Christianity was still a *Freethinker* pastime, but in the world of liberal theology and TV religion it was a different game. Although the privileges of the established church in Britain were constantly criticised, Catholicism was seen as a greater threat from a worldwide perspective. Hochhuth's play *The Representative*, presented at first in Berlin by Piscator, stirred up heated arguments about the papal attitude to fascism and Nazism. The play tells of Pius XII's failure to take any steps to condemn Hitler's death camps, despite urgent representations. Hochhuth alleges this was due to the Concordat and a fear of communist victory. A Catholic outcry and attempt to suppress the play produced much comment in the *Freethinker.*

Another war-time Catholic evil was raised by a proposal for the canonisation of Cardinal Archbishop Alojzije Stepinac. In an article "For Stepinac — A Sainthood", Eva Ebury described how he had conceived "the nightmare of a Catholic Independent Croatia". She continued:

> Using the infiltration and propaganda powers of Catholic Action and its affiliated organisations, Great Brotherhood of Crusaders, Catholic Student Association, Great Sisterhood of Crusaders and the like, he persuaded the faithful that it would be a good deed, and in the highest interests of Croatia and the Catholic Church, to kill or convert the Serbs, and to exterminate the Jews. In the words of Pavelich's Minister of Education, "We shall kill one part of the Serbs, we shall transport another, and the rest of them will be enforced to embrace the Roman Catholic religion". How well these pious aims were accomplished is summed up by Monica Farrell *(Ravening Wolves)* in the statement that "nearly 70,000 of the 80,000 Jews in the entire country were killed or forced to flee, their property being confiscated. 240,000 Serbs became Byzantine Rite Roman Catholics through forced conversion on pain of death". Serbian church properties were seized and turned over to Roman Catholic converts by authority of Stepinac...
>
> Now Archbishop Stepinac has died branded as a murderer and traitor by the Yugoslavia Court of Justice, and mourned by Pope and Hierarchy, and that faith-deluded flock who hear only the travesty of truth permitted by the Vatican. (25 March, 1960.)

Avro Manhattan's attacks on the Catholic Church were quoted and promoted in the *Freethinker,* but his book *Religious Terror in Ireland* was criticised as being the work of a Paisleyite. He replied: "While admitting that I am a friend of Mr. Paisley, I utterly reject the allegation that I am one of his followers, and even less, supporters... I am as opposed to Catholic intellectual impertinence as to Protestant biblical sub-culture." (16 January, 1971.)

The political ambition of the Vatican was much suspected by freethinkers and the candidacy of the Catholic, John F. Kennedy, for the Presidency of the USA caused Walter L. Arnstein to ask in an article on "The Kennedy Candidacy": "Would Senator Kennedy as President be in any sense a pawn of the Vatican?" (20 May, 1960.) Opinions varied, but on balance the danger to freethought was thought no greater than that presented by Vice-President Nixon who "introduced a gratuitous barb aimed at Freethinkers". "There was only one way in which religion might become an issue, he said. That would be 'if a candidate had no religion at all'." (20 May, 1960.) When Kennedy was assassinated the death of a liberal was regretted, but the temptation to allow martyrdom to bestow sainthood was also avoided.

The running sore of Catholic entanglement with fascism and fear of Catholic political power did not blind freethinkers to the merits of "A Liberal Pope", as John XXIII was described on his death. In a front-page article Ridley said:

> Pope John, both in his general attitude and specifically in his recent encyclical letter on peace, appears definitely to have modified the intransigent attitude of his immediate predecessors towards the international situation in general and towards the Cold War in particular. Unlike the belligerent Piuses, who in and out of season preached a "Holy War" against atheistic Bolshevism and all its Satanic works, he envisaged and encouraged a peaceful solution for the great ideological conflict of our time between the rival social systems of East and West...
>
> For this, and for other reasons, Humanists will deplore the passing of this undoubtedly liberal pope, and will hope that the College of Cardinals (whether illuminated or not by the hypothetical Holy Spirit who is supposed to make a speciality in presiding over papal elections) will have sufficient good sense to elect a similarly broadminded prelate as his successor, rather than another reactionary. (14 June, 1963.)

Subsequent developments led Barbara Smoker, the ex-Catholic President of the National Secular Society, who often commented upon Catholic affairs, to declare "The Pope is Now a Protestant". In an article provoked by a rebellious priest refusing to use the vernacular mass, she said:

> The final arbiter in matters of faith is now more likely to be the Bible, freely interpreted, than the authority of Catholic tradition, and the final arbiter in matters of morals is more likely to be the individual conscience than the authority of the hierarchy. The incantations and making secret gestures over the altar, has given place to a participant congregation. (October, 1976.)

The one area in which Catholics and Protestants offered a steadfastly different approach, at least at the official level, was that of personal morality. The *Freethinker* for two decades castigated the Catholic Church for its record in areas such as birth control, abortion, and homosexuality.

Protestantism became woollier and woollier until distinguishing between a liberal theologian and a non-Christian was like telling one sheep from the next. The "modern" Christian was not unknown in Foote's day, but in the sixties became sufficiently prominent to baffle even Christian supporters. In 1960 the Dean of St. Pauls said that the Thirty-Nine-Articles were out of date; twenty years later a Cambridge theologian, Don Cupitt, questioned whether Jesus was the incarnation. (It was rare for resignation to accompany collapse of belief.) In between the Bishop of Woolwich tried to be "Honest to God". Colin McCall pointed out that John Robinson's ideas were not new to readers of European theologians such as Tillich, Bonhoeffer and Bultman, but said:

> Nevertheless, it must come as a shock to ordinary members of the Church of England that one of their own bishops should so openly express his rejection of the traditional conceptions of God and Jesus Christ... And, indeed, although Dr. Robinson may be trying to be honest to God, his

> book is rather more a rescue operation than a search for truth...
>
> *Honest to God* is, it must be agreed, a courageous book for a bishop to write. At the same time its philosophy is unsound and it is hopelessly ambiguous. One can only assume that, while intellectually with the atheists, Dr. Robinson finds it impossible to sever his emotional attachment to Christianity and chooses instead radically to change it. But as he himself is aware, he has "erred in not being nearly radical enough". The logical step is to atheism. (5 April, 1963.)

Some Christians responded by moving the other way and there were revivals of fundamentalist, evangelical Christianity. "This Billy Graham Business" was the title of an article that queried the impact of the travelling American gospeller — grandfather of the born-again movement:

> Scratch under the surface of Billy Graham's 'successes' and you find that there is nothing underneath. He gets a temporary emotional response only from those prone to make a display of "conversion" when the occasion arises. They turn out to be church members already, curious youngsters and mentally unstable and retarded subjects, when the results are analysed. (8 April, 1955.)

At the end of its first hundred years it is surprising to find an almost medieval example of the abuses of religion with an exorcism case in Germany. Two Roman Catholic priests were tried and found guilty of negligence after a young woman theology student who believed she was possessed by the devil died of hunger and exhaustion — "The rites of exorcism had been administered to her 67 times before she died, and she had been refusing food and drink in the advanced stages." The *Freethinker* claimed that it was time for the churches to repudiate the practice of exorcism: "Too many tragedies can occur, when the vulnerable or sick have their difficulties compounded with evil aspects of religion rather than being given medical treatment or sane, compassionate counselling." (May, 1978.)

National Secular Society members returned to the streets to protest at some of the more absurd manifestations of Christianity. The popularity of the musical show "Jesus Christ Superstar" gave the opportunity for an attack on the Jesus Movement. A leaflet headed "Jesus Christ Supersham" was distributed outside the theatre; the mini-revival of the Jesus movement was described as "even more anti-intellectual and inane" than the revivals of Moody and Sankey or Billy Graham. (12 August, 1972.)

The organisers of the "London Festival for Jesus", the Nationwide Festival of Light, were attacked in a leaflet "Festival of Twilight". The leaflet was distributed at events organised to celebrate the so-called "Dunkirk-Miracle 72". It said:

> Those who make preposterous claims about God's intervention seem to forget that before Dunkirk millions of prayers had been offered up for peace; war was declared. And after Dunkirk God appears to have gone off duty, allowing British cities to be bombed and millions of his Chosen People to be murdered in concentration camps. (2 September, 1972.)

Energetic Campaigning

The mid-sixties were years of vigorous activity for the National Secular Society, with a high number of public meetings. A wide number of well-known personalities contributed to humanist campaigns. An energetic campaign to fight school religion included a Secular Education Month with a large public meeting at which Harold Pinter said the basic question was not whether religion was right or wrong but whether it should be imposed, and Margaret Knight declared "Our ultimate aim should be the ending of religious instruction in county schools". (18 December, 1964.) Secularists were discouraged when the Minister of Education, Mr. Edward Short, said that he "intends to preserve compulsory provision of religious education in county schools, and the daily act of worship in the new education act." (25 January, 1969.) A few years later a deputation from the National Secular Society presented their case to Mrs. Thatcher, who was then Minister of Education. The *Freethinker* reported that she listened courteously, but said that "no major change was envisaged at present". (4 December, 1971.)

The old argument about whether to keep religion out of schools entirely or whether to trust schools and RE teachers to present children with a mixture of comparative religion, atheist arguments and moral education was very much alive. The controversy created hard feeling when the *Freethinker* described the British Humanist Association's wholehearted support of a Social Morality Council report on Religious Education as "A Sell Out". (The *Freethinker* always gave space to opposing views, however heated.). When Reg Prentice, another Minister of Education, gave an opportunity for legislation to raise the capital grant for aided and special-grant church schools by 5 per cent to 85 per cent, the *Freethinker* headlined "Government Sell-Out to Churches". (August, 1974.)

A public meeting with the subject of "Religious Education: the New Indoctrination" included a trenchant speech from Brigid Brophy. She opened: "I should like to make it clear that my reason for considering Jesus Christ an unsuitable person to preside over the schooling of the nation's children has nothing to do with the story that he was born to an unmarried mother, under (according to tradition) the age of 16, in socio-economic class four..."

The speech concluded with an appeal for honesty:

> At present we force our schools to tell children a tale about how baby Jesus was born to an unmarried virgin and a god and a star magically located the place where he lay. And when the children ask why they should believe that, we can give them only the resounding inane answer "Because Parliament says God says so". I can think of no quicker or neater way of discrediting, in children's eyes, the whole apparatus of civilisation, intellectual, moral and aesthetic, which is what we profess to be trying to hand on to them in their schooling.
>
> Children deserve better from us than an education subverted on its

> home ground by the superimposition of anti-reasonable values issued on non-existent authority. They deserve, in fact, our honesty. (November, 1974.)

The *Freethinker* was useful to publicise full accounts of the many meetings held during this period of activity. Among the meetings supported by prominent individuals was one on "Capital Punishment", which was addressed by Canon John Collins, Louis Blom-Cooper and the Right Hon. Kenneth Younger. Opponents of capital punishment were given useful information by a *Freethinker* interview with Mrs. Lilian Bentley, mother of Derek Bentley, hanged in 1953, although entirely innocent of murder. (11 September, 1971.)

At the National Secular Society Centenary Dinner in 1966 the speakers were David Tribe, Brigid Brophy, Michael Foot and Charles Bradlaugh Bonner. Booklets were published, press statements issued, and submissions to government and other bodies made — for example to the Archbishop's Commission on Church and State and to the Public Schools Commission in 1967. Reading the bound volumes and talking to participants at the time, I am given the impression of heady days. A very wide range of interest extended beyond anti-Christian propaganda to pamphlets on Birth Control and the Rights of Old People. The *Freethinker* also published details of humanist support for a school in Bechuanaland.

Sexuality and Humanism

A meeting in 1967 on "Humanism, Christianity and Sex" at which Leo Abse, Brigid Brophy and the Rev. Edward Carpenter spoke, delineates an area that was prominent in the *Freethinker* in the sixties and seventies. The subject could be overdone for some readers. After an issue which contained articles on "Sex is Not Smut", "A Study of Sexuality" and "Sex, Doctors and God" complaints came in, for example:

> As a lifelong Secularist on the wrong side of 70 years, I note with an increasing dismay over the last few months the deterioration of the FREETHINKER as an effective weapon in the fight against organised Christianity in Europe and those even more absurd beliefs abroad... our main opponent is the Roman Catholic Church... The present seeming obsession with sex, abortion, and so-called "free art"... will not get us much further along our proper road. (30 June, 1967.)

Instead of constantly bemoaning the need for reform the *Freethinker* was able to praise the architects of real reform with the legalisation of abortion, of homosexual acts between consenting adults, and more rational divorce arrangements. The problem was then to become one of resisting a backlash against reform — especially the vigorous attempts to repeal or modify the 1967 Abortion Act. Rapid changes in social morals are reflected in the *Freethinker* columns. Although feminists might see it as only a beginning, the position of women in society was radically altered. The churches were slow to notice this and the Dean of Llandaff was reported as saying, "I have known women sidesmen in church, but that surely is an admission of failure." (January, 1973.). Anglican leaders eventually had to face demands from C. of E. grass roots for equality for women and permission for their ordination. A statement from Barbara Smoker, who became President of the National Secular Society in 1972, showed why freethinkers and feminists had often been ranged against Christians, for God, she said, was presented by Christians as "The Original Male Chauvinist Pig": "Christianity and other orthodox religions are, and always have been, essentially anti-feminist." (June, 1973.)

In 1967 the *Freethinker* used the headline "Abortion Law — Reformed" and declared: "This is a victory for ALRA (Abortion Law Reform Association) which campaigned so long for saner legislation and a victory for the Humanist movement which saw in the Cause for which ALRA fought a truly Humanist objective." (10 November, 1967.) When the anti-abortion lobby attempted to reverse the law, Barbara Smoker described God as "the greatest abortionist of all", "being deliberately responsible for spontaneous abortion (miscarriages), the incidence of which far exceeds that of induced abortions, even today". She suggested that the anti-abortion lobby should adopt the prayer "O, thou great Abortionist! Thine is the monopoly of righteous abortion, for ever and ever. Amen." (July, 1974.)

Propaganda to repeal or modify the 1967 Abortion Act fell into the hands of lobbyists and MPs in the form of a book, *Babies for Burning* by Susan Kentish and Michael Litchfield. The book accused abortion agencies and doctors of encouraging unnecessary abortion and ill-treating clients and live foeti. The *Freethinker* immediately reviewed the book with scepticism declaring that the emotive phraseology was "bound to raise doubts as to the veracity of their assurance that they undertook the project with 'no pre-conceived notions..... dispassionately, in complete isolation and detachment'." When the *Freethinker* was threatened with libel action by the authors, the editor W. McIlroy roundly stated that the *Freethinker* "will not be muzzled" — despite the potential serious legal costs. (May, 1975.) The case was dropped and the authors later withdrew many of their allegations as a result of exposure in the press and action in courts.

Freethinkers do not *favour* abortion: they favour the individual's right to make this difficult choice taking into account the feelings and circumstances of those involved. Adoption and abolition of the concept of illegitimacy have also been championed by freethinkers as answers to unplanned pregnancies. An article entitled "Illegitimacy" by "Edmund" called for a change of attitude and blamed the Christian churches for "the predicament of the unmarried mother and her bastard child". (8 July, 1960.) Atheists were discriminated against by adoption agencies and freethinkers supported an Agnostic (later Independent) Adoption

Society, which was sympathetic to those of any religious belief or none.

The Sunday People ran an article, signed by John Junor, which used the headline "YOU ARE NOT FIT TO ADOPT ONE OF OUR CHILDREN" and argued that "on the basis of the interests of the children concerned they should go only to Christian homes". A front-page *Freethinker* article by Margaret McIlroy said:

> The most important point about religion and adoption is never even referred to by *The People*. Though a ban on non-Christians is operated by most large adoption societies, there are other ways of acquiring a child, and many non-believers have in fact adopted children successfully...
>
> *The People* says that the children are the ones who should be considered. It concludes "Their happiness comes first. The rights of atheists and agnostics must take second place". We could agree with *The People* if it would add, "The rights of the Roman Catholic Church must take second place too". (19 April, 1963.)

In the same month there was comment on the debate of Leo Abse's Bill to reform divorce law: "The Church leaders are behaving true to form in condemning the divorce-by-consent clause in Mr. Leo Abse's private Bill now before Parliament". Leading clerics signed a statement declaring that "it would undermine the basic understanding of marriage as a life-long union if the principle were introduced that a marriage could be terminated by the desire of the partners". (19 April, 1963.) That Bill was lost, but reform was later successfully brought in.

Although freethinkers had always denied the equation of freethought and free love, the *Freethinker* joined in the profound questioning of marriage taking place in the sixties. An article by Maurice Hill, "Patterns of Living and Loving", spoke of the need to escape from "the old repressive 'morality', removing the stigma attached to 'living in sin' and illegitimacy, and learning to accept pre-marital sex, homosexual behaviour, and sexual freedom for children and adolescents... The family as we now know it is not necessarily the best arrangement for some individuals". (4 October, 1969.)

Sexual relations between adults and children was a very controversial frontier of the discussion of morality and social reform. When an article by Antony Grey, the former director of the Albany Trust and a leading campaigner for the successful legalisation of consenting homosexual acts between adults, asked "Paedophiles — Are we dodging the issue?" there was a heated correspondence. The *Freethinker* has always stood for the rational discussion of taboo subjects — knowing that its readers will expect to encounter articles with which they do not agree.

Freedom of Speech

Opposition to censorship remained firm at a time when freedoms were being denied and gained in the courts. The acquittal of the publishers of *Lady Chatterley's Lover* from an obscenity charge was welcomed "by all who concern themselves with freedom of expression". (11 November, 1960.) Many subsequent cases were reported in the *Freethinker*, including prosecutions concerning *Last Exit to Brooklyn* and the counter-culture magazine *Oz*. Another counter-culture magazine, *International Times*, was prosecuted for printing homosexual personal contact ads. The *Freethinker* commented: Surely, now that this much-beleaguered and long-suffering section of society has at last been allowed to exist legally, they can be permitted to advertise for friends in the same way as heterosexuals". (10 May, 1969.) After the *Little Red School Book*, which gave clear, honest sexual information to teenagers, was prosecuted, the National Secular Society invited its publisher, Richard Handyside, to be the Guest of Honour at the Annual Dinner. When Lord Longford went ferreting for pornography and wrote up his experiences as the Longford Report, the *Freethinker* irreverently headlined: "Oh, Lord Longford: Get Stuffed!"

A free speech issue of great contention was raised by racist behaviour in society. The extent to which people should be given freedom to say obnoxious things is always controversial. An early (unsuccessful) attempt by Sir Leslie Plummer to introduce a Bill to prohibit expression of racial prejudice was opposed by the President of the National Secular Society, at a National Council of Civil Liberties conference on "Anti-Semitism and Racial Incitement", because "of the difficulty of enforcement and the existing plethora of censorial legislation". David Tribe forcefully expressed the case for free speech:

> The proposed measure will surely be condemned by liberal opinion as treating Fascism with Fascism. We do not believe that ideas, however foolish or dangerous, can be disposed of by driving them underground. Rather should they be dragged out into the open to be scorched by the pure light of reason. Religious and race dogmatists have a case to put. It is, in our opinion, a false one, indeed a revolting one. But we shall certainly be creating a very dangerous precedent if we deny them the right to put it. (18 March, 1960.)

This view was put to the test when an article supporting Enoch Powell's phobias about racial minorities was printed (thus confirming that the *Freethinker* would print views opposite to its principles, just as it had occasionally included the writings of clergymen in the past). The article caused protest from readers and the alternative view was, of course, immediately put: an article on Powell and "Powellism" described him as "a racialist, believing as he does that any movement in Britain to a thoroughly multi-racial society would be retrograde". Powell and those who supported the right of racialists to free speech were attacked: "Racialism is not a view, an opinion, a case — it is an obscenity. To allow the racialist a platform is to make him respectable, to concede that he has a point that should be considered..." (22 February, 1969.)

The defence of the right to publish controversial material emerged in a major blasphemy case. The many changes in almost 100 years between the prosecution of G.W. Foote and the editor of *Gay News* for blasphemy were not sufficient to have abolished the common law offence of vilification of a non-existent entity. A private prosecution by Lady Birdwood had been brought against the stage play, *Council of Love*, which depicted God, Jesus, and Satan as comic figures on the stage in 1971. The case failed on a technicality. The public were reminded of the existence of the law of blasphemy by the Archbishop of Canterbury and Mrs. Whitehouse when the Swedish film-maker, Jess Thorsen, said in 1976 that he was going to make a film about the sex life of Jesus.

In 1977 Mary Whitehouse brought a private prosecution against *Gay News* for publishing a poem by James Kirkup, "The Love That Dares To Speak Its Name", in which a homosexual centurion speaks of his love for the crucified Jesus Christ and recalls the passionate vigour of Christ's sexual love for other men. The poem was essentially Christian in its attempt to show that Christ's love embraced all forms of loving. Just as some freethinkers had found Foote's use of cartoons offensive, so some freethinkers considered Kirkup's poem in poor taste. The National Secular Society said the prosecution "threatens to put the clock back to the days of Christian tyranny". (January, 1977.) The editor of *Gay News*, Denis Lemon, was found guilty and sentenced to 9 months imprisonment suspended for 18 months, and fined £500. The President of the National Secular Society, Barbara Smoker, said that "The first successful prosecution for blasphemy in 56 years must make Britain the laughing stock of the civilised world". (August, 1977.)

The Committee Against Blasphemy Law was founded and issued a statement signed by prominent individuals such as J.B. Priestley, Margaret Drabble, Brigid Brophy, twenty MPs, and prominent Christians such as the Dean of Manchester and Prof. G.W. Lampe. At a rally in Trafalgar Square at the time of the appeal, W. McIlroy, the former *Freethinker* editor and Hon. Secretary of CABL, was a speaker. The appeal failed. A copy of the *Freethinker* from 1922 was handed to the appeal judges, because their own records of the case against J.W. Gott were missing. (March, 1978.)

Denis Lemon became the Guest of Honour at the National Secular Society Annual Dinner. In proposing a toast to him for his courage in the face of censorship, Maureen Duffy said:

> We have reached a truly ludicrous state where atheists have to try to stop one religious faction from pounding another, while at the same time we are accused of destroying that strange substance the nation's moral fibre. This substance, the nation's moral fibre, I have always seen as a kind of potting compost in which the luscious weeds of persecution, repression and sanctimoniousness can be nurtured. (April, 1978.)

A bizarre footnote to the blasphemy case was provided by a prosecution of the former editor of the *Freethinker*, W. McIlroy, for contravening a Post Office Act by sending the allegedly blasphemous poem through the post. He was fined £50.

Mrs. Mary Whitehouse came into prominence, some years before the blasphemy case, after founding a "Clean Up TV Campaign" later to become the National Viewers and Listeners Association, which has always been a Christian propaganda organisation rather than a representative audience "consumer association". The campaign was launched by the wife of a Staffordshire rector and Mrs. Whitehouse, a schoolmistress in Wolverhampton, both known as militant members of the Moral Rearmament Group. Its original title was "Women of Britain Clean up TV Campaign" and its first manifesto began "We men and women of Britain believe in a Christian way of life..." The *Freethinker* gave out early warning signals: "We feel that this campaign is a definite threat to the expression of liberal and humanist views on television and radio and consequently we are writing to our local MPs, to the Director General of the BBC and to the Postmaster-General asking that they resist these attempts to impose censorship". (9 April, 1965.)

Mrs. Whitehouse was described as "Public Detergent No. 1" in an article by Kit Mouat in which the morals campaigner was accused of ignoring the real obscenities of our time: "Does Mrs. Whitehouse, in her purple turban and pearls, care about the bereaved families in Vietnam, the homeless in our own country, the Africans who are treated as second-rate citizens in order that the greed, power or just the ability of white people shall be fulfilled..." (17 December, 1965.)

The attempt to muzzle a liberal and humanist media would not have been necessary if the BBC had not begun to "escape from the Reith strait-jacket". Evidence of this was seen in a report that a ban on references to religion, royalty, politicians and sex in light entertainment was lifted, "giving them the same freedom as 'That Was The Week That Was', which escaped the ban by coming under the Talks and Current Affairs Department". (25 January, 1963.) The satirical programme TWTWTW provoked 100 phone calls of protest when a religious satirical sketch showed three clerics singing about "Togetherness" and then walking off in different directions: "Christian television viewers, so used to having their cherished beliefs protected by the B.B.C., are finding it hard to adapt themselves". (1 February, 1963.)

More important than satirising religion was the unequivocal presentation of the atheist, humanist position. Margaret Knight created a furore when in 1955 she gave a series of talks on "Morals Without Religion": "On January 5, 1955, broadcasting history was made when basic religious beliefs were allowed to be challenged in plain terms, and the B.B.C. became, in the affronted eyes of the faithful, a hotbed of Atheism overnight — and if the pun be excused, over Knight". (11 March, 1955.) The press screamed headlines like "Godless Radio Repeat Scandalises Nation" from the *Daily Sketch* and "Take this woman off the air" from a church newspaper. The outcry greatly increased the interest in her views and she was much in demand as a public speaker throughout the country.

It became less startling for humanists to present their views on the media. In October 1963, David Tribe was one of a panel of three who discussed "Life After Death" with a group of young people in the ITV *Sunday Break* programme. In 1965 a peak Saturday morning radio time was given to a series of 6 talks by well-known humanists including A.J. Ayer, James Hemming, Lord Francis-Williams and Lord Willis. Despite a steady trickle of humanist voices in the media, freethinkers cannot be happy they are often used as a foil for debate in religious programmes, that the B.B.C. makes daily assumptions about the Christianity of the nation, and that to this day the Religious Affairs Department is a vigorous part of the B.B.C.

Worldwide

Increased communication has given greater prominence in the press and electronic media to worldwide issues (albeit often perfunctory, lacking analysis, and concentrating on "trouble spots" to the exclusion of large areas of the world). The *Freethinker* has increased its coverage of worldwide events in the last twenty years. To begin fairly close to home — Ireland has been the subject of anguished comment (as it was in Foote's day). Before the worst of the troubles exploded again in Belfast, an article on "Belfast 1960" was published:

> Social relations between Roman Catholic and Protestant teenagers seem to be almost non-existent; neither group seeks, nor is desirous of the others' company. Compared with teenagers of earlier years, the present generation is not so readily provoked into active violence, but the sparks still smoulder and with vigorous fanning might easily flare up. In isolated cases gangs are formed and deliberately seek out the opposing side, then violence does take place. But then, to be fair, these gangs, and the dupes who constitute them, don't necessarily need a religious issue to brutalise them. And the magistrates and police of both denominations take an equally serious view of both sides. (21 October, 1960.)

Nigel Sinnott, an editor of the *Freethinker* who paid much attention to the Irish situation, wrote that "the British Government's decision to prorogue Stormont and institute direct rule in Northern Ireland from Westminster may shed a faint ray of hope upon a political situation that should have been faced more sensibly half a century ago." He saw the situation "not in terms of religious sectarianism *per se*, but as an old colonial and communal situation with fossilized seventeenth-century political overtones... Religion has, however, played a crucial part in ensuring that the two original communities, Planter and Gael, remained at loggerheads by virtue of penal legislation, discouraging intermarriage, and by separating and marking out their descendants from birth by means of sectarian 'education'."

The article was headed "Ireland: A New Easter Lily?" and concluded: "For fifty years Irishmen have worn white lilies at Easter-time; Unionists still sing of the Orange Lily-O. It is time that a blossom of a different hue was given a chance to bloom". (1 April, 1972.)

The *Freethinker* focussed upon the religious dimension of a major conflict — the war in Vietnam. In 1963 the National Secular Society protested to the Vietnam Ambassador in London about his Catholic-dominated Government's policy towards the Buddhist majority in that country. After a Buddhist monk burned himself to death to draw attention to Catholic intolerance, a *Freethinker* front page referred to the worsening situation with martial law imposed and postponement of elections. There was a reference to "the fervent Catholicism of the ruling family" and the fact that Washington and the Vatican were disturbed by "their respective 'image' in South-East Asia and the world at large". The *Freethinker* article said:

> Certainly the endless war against the northern Communists is a factor to be considered, even if it is being fought mainly by the Americans. But perhaps, at long last, the United States is realising the blunder of bolstering a hated Roman Catholic ruling family as a "bulwark against Communism", realising that it is, in fact, having the opposite effect. After all, seventy-five per cent of Vietnamese are Buddhists. (6 September, 1963.)

Rigid Communist control of the Eastern bloc was criticised after the Hungarian revolution in 1956. Colin McCall wrote in "Hungary: An Attempted Assessment":

> Most seemingly reliable reporters, however, insist that there was a genuine people's uprising against a dictatorial regime; not merely nationalistic — though that element was present — but also demanding greater freedom... Our admiration and sympathy go out to the magnificent people of Hungary in their struggle for freedom and their terrible sufferings. (28 December, 1956.)

The National Secular Society had sent a letter of protest to the Soviet Ambassador in London on 6 November:

> The National Secular Society believes that the Roman Catholic Church is the greatest menace in the world today and constantly says so in public. It does not wish to see the re-establishment of papal power in Poland, Hungary, or elsewhere. Nevertheless, it firmly believes that each country has a right to determine its own form of government. (28 December, 1956.)

A struggle for freedom in the leading country of the so-called "free" bloc took place in America. Madalyn Murray's fight to remove prayers and religious readings from schools because they were unconstitutional was successfully taken to the U.S. Supreme Court in 1963. The *Freethinker* headlined "Madalyn Murray — Victory" and wrote:

> The decision following last year's ruling that the reading of a non-denomination prayer in the schools of New York state was unconstitutional must be regarded as a powerful reassertion of the separation of church and state in the USA and is in fact a victory for Secularism. It must also be regarded as a great victory for Mrs. Murray and her sons (achieved at great personal inconvenience and even suffering) and for the Pennsylvanian Unitarian appellants. (28 June, 1963.)

Madalyn Murray's "declaration of faith" delivered to the American

Rationalist Federation on 25 August, 1962 in St. Louis was quoted, while the final appeal was taking place:

> Ours is a time when successful struggle against this reactionary philosophy ("idealist" and God-believing) requires more than a petulant argument over the authorship of the Gospels, more than a negative attack on the totalitarian and monolithic authoritarianism of conventional religion, but rather an aggressive action programme to spread the positive philosophy of materialism. (15 March, 1963.)

Another rationalist campaigner to suffer for his beliefs was Eddie Roux, the Chairman of the South African Rationalist Association and Professor of Botany at the University of Witwatersrand, Johannesburg. He was also a *Freethinker* contributor. In 1965 he was banned "from entering any educational institution, from teaching and writing, and confined to the Johannesburg area" by the South African Government. He was accused of communist activities though he had had no association with the Communist Party for thirty years. His academic career ended and the South African Rationalist Association and its journal *The Rationalist* faced severe difficulties without his support. The *Freethinker* commented: "The Association had a following in university circles and its organ had for some time been printed partly in Afrikaans. Disseminating rationalist ideas among the Afrikaaners may well have been regarded as a sin by the South African Government, as well as by the powerful fundamentalist Dutch Reformed Church". (15 January, 1965.)

The *Freethinker* was a fierce opponent of apartheid and the tyranny used to sustain it. The National Secular Society sent a letter to the South African High Commissioner at the time of the Sharpeville massacre, expressing its "deep-felt horrors at the terrible massacre of coloured South Africans at Sharpeville, and protests most strongly at this latest example of the ghastly folly of the South African Government's racial policy". (1 April, 1960.)

After the massacre of black Africans at Soweto, an article by Barry Duke, "The Much Deformed Church", attacked the role of the Dutch Reformed Church: "The powderkeg that was Soweto and its sister ghettoes has — to South Africa's cost and eternal discredit — finally erupted into a holocaust of unprecedented violence... Is it fair to blame the Church for actions of the Government? Certainly it is; in South Africa Church and State are synonomous". (August, 1976.)

The continuing interest in India was seen in an assessment by Govind Deodhekar of Nehru's work at the time of his death. Nehru was said to be "probably the only Prime Minister (outside the Communist world) to openly profess his agnostic or rationalist views — and to include in his will a specific rejection of religion... Nehru was the only one of the national leaders to realise that the struggle for freedom and democracy in India was part of the world-wide struggle against imperialism and Fascism". (12 June, 1964.)

The dangers of a sectarian religious state were illustrated by the case of Pakistan. After the hanging of Bhutto, an article entitled "Whither Pakistan?" considered the future of the Islamic state: "The chance of such a sobering up of the Muslim mood are not very bright. The Islamic revolution is very fresh and Saudi oil money is still a potent factor... Islamic fundamentalism and revivalism are only a blind alley leading to a brick wall on which one can only hurl oneself to frustration and self-destruction". (June, 1979.)

An article about "The Islamic Republic of Iran" by "An Indian Rationalist", stated that "In the fullness of time the realisation must come that a modern people cannot run their affairs on the basis of a medieval penal code or a seventh-century 'revelation'." (March, 1979.) Many subsequent items about atrocities in Iran were to show how far away that fullness of time was.

Militancy and Humanism

Although militant, fundamentalist religion had not yet vanished from the world, arguments about the need for militant atheist secularism could still be heated. They were not new — Foote and Holyoake had differed sharply over the need for militancy. In an article "Why Be Militant?" by G.I. Bennett, tolerance was urged:

> For my own part, I want freedom to think and freedom to express my ideas and I will readily concede the same freedom to others — mindful as I am that religious institutions in their heyday did not grant that freedom to us heretics, and would not today but for the work of pioneer movements like ours. I trust I shall always condemn forthrightly what I conceive to be evil — especially any wanton curtailment of human life, liberty and happiness —but I shall not be perturbed about others holding views opposite to mine, whether or not they are in the majority. So long, that is, as they do not try to enforce my conformity. (19 April, 1957.)

The currency of the word "humanism" gave impetus to an emphasis on the open society, ethical concern, philosophical debate and dialogue with Christians. Attempts to categorise the National Secular Society as solely composed of old-fashioned Bible-bashers and the British Humanist Association as the new-wave positive ethicists would be a gross over-simplification, for each organisation contained much diversity and there was overlap of membership and activists. However, there was strong criticism of a dialogue between representatives of the Roman Catholic Church and the International Humanist and Ethical Union, at which H.J. Blackham was the BHA representative. The *Freethinker* said on its front page: "We are not in the least surprised that the Secretariat for Unbelievers should have sought this meeting: the Roman Catholic Church has a great deal to gain and nothing to lose by even temporary ceasefire in its losing battle against freethought. But what can be the motives of the IHEU? To put it bluntly what have they intellectually in common with men who eat their God in church each Sunday?" (10 September, 1965.) Heated and considered comments came in letters and a symposium of reactions. Barbara Smoker took a reasonable middle ground:

> No good can come from sheer abuse of the Churches, and still less from abuse of each other. From the reaction to the talks between the BHA and Vatican representatives, anyone would think that all the officers of the BHA had submitted to baptism! Diplomatic dialogues are the normal procedure between nations engaged in a cold war, and even minor points of agreement can have good social results. Besides, genuine knowledge and understanding of the enemy are far more likely to win battles than is ignorance fed upon one's own propaganda. (13 May, 1966.)

Further ill-feeling arose when a *Freethinker* front page criticised the British Humanist Association as an organisation "heavily loaded with well-educated middle-class people" and said "our narcissistically Intellectual Humanists are disinclined to fraternise with working-class people". (20 January, 1967.) A riposte about "the essential sterility of secularism" fanned the flames of antagonism. One suspects that, as ever, personal animosities played their part as well as differences of principle, but there has always been an honourable difference of emphasis between non-religious moralists and anti-religious activists. It re-appeared in another guise in the discussion of "religious humanism" in the seventies. Religious humanism seemed no more destined to acquire a large following than did positivism in the nineteenth century. C. Morey wrote in an article looking at "The Case of Religious Humanism": "One of the perennial debates within the humanist movement is whether it is desirable or profitable vigorously to oppose the Churches and their gods, or whether an alliance with those Christians thought to be more in sympathy with humanist ideas might prove useful, indeed, might prove the way ahead, a new Reformation, giving the spiritual impetus so thought to be lacking at the present time". (June, 1975.)

Secularism still retained its role as a critique of religion. The *Freethinker* was particularly diligent in exposing the cults and sects which mushroomed at a time of decline of institutional religion. The 'Rev' Moon and his Unification Church were criticised long before their indoctrination techniques became the subject of a court case. W. McIlroy interviewed a supporter of the Divine Light Mission, led by a podgy Indian fifteen-year-old, the Guru Maharishi Ji. He found trying to pin down their beliefs like "trying to trap bubbles in a wind tunnel". (January, 1973.) An article "Children of God: The Dupes of Moses David" by McIlroy, declared:

> We do not seek to deprive religionists of the right to disseminate their views however silly and pernicious they may be. But it is no restriction on intellectual freedom to prevent the Children of God from fleecing tourists, shoppers and travellers; on the contrary, their fund-raising activities may provoke a hostile public reaction and authoritarian elements to demand an end to all street activities. (May, 1974.)

The outstanding example of the way such sects could destroy their followers was the tragedy of the mass suicide of hundreds of disciples of

Jim Jones's Peoples Temple in Guyana. The *Freethinker* pointed out: "The fringe religions do not differ essentially from Christianity, which is itself based on an alleged suicide by someone who felt he had a special mission to be crucified". (January, 1979.)

A public debate between Barbara Smoker and a leader of the International Society for Krishna Consciousness was as colourful as some of the debates with fundamentalists in the nineteenth century. The temperature of the debate was characterised by a Hare Krishna supporter who at one point threatened Barbara Smoker with what he claimed was a gun. An article, "His Grace Hare Krishna Das and Her Logic Miss Barbara Smoker" speculated on the value of the debate:

> Was it worth it? In every age it has been important to challenge the deist claims of religious groups. Today debate with Christianity is rather like unravelling wool, or — to change metaphors — arguing with a chameleon: now the incarnation of Jesus is a myth, now it isn't; now hell is a negative state of mind, now it is a positive tug into the forces of evil. The more fundamental religions — Eastern as well as Western — at least put forward propositions which have sufficient consistency and clarity to debate. (July, 1979.)

Conclusion

The dual role of secularism in criticising religion and propounding social reform has been maintained throughout its hundred years. It was restated in David Tribe's statement on the Second Hundred Years of the National Secular Society: "The National Secular Society intends to fight even harder in the next hundred years for a national secular society, which will stress our common humanity and have no established churches, no official religious ceremonies nationally or locally, and no formal oath. In this open society of the future, personal beliefs will vary, but the community will foster communal well being". (17 February, 1967.)

The critique of Christianity was authoritatively expressed in an article by Margaret Knight, "Christianity: the Debit Account" (later published as a leaflet):

> The indictment against Christianity is formidable; and when Christians today grow indignant about obscurantism, intolerance and ideological persecution in Communist countries, they would be well to remember that the Church in the ages of faith had a far worse record. This is not to deny that the Church has also done much good; so, too, has Communism. But the crucial factor, surely is that, as Voltaire remarked, men who believe in absurdities will commit atrocities. One of the best ways to improve men's behaviour is to enlighten their minds: and today, against the strong opposition of the Church and the Establishment, Scientific Humanism is attempting to do just that. (29 January, 1965.)

The vision and realism of the twofold secularist programme — countering religion and constructing reform — are as relevant as ever for the next 100 years of the *Freethinker.*

A survey and stock-taking of secularism and freethought in the modern world were to be found in a special centenary issue of the *Freethinker* (May 1981), which contained contributions from distinguished writers such as Brigid Brophy, Barbara Wootton, Hermann Bondi, Dora Russell, Maureen Duffy and Edward Blishen.

Michael Foot, leader of the Labour Party, in the same year delivered a lecture to the Leicester Secular Society on the occasion of the centenary of the foundation of its Secular Hall. His subject was "Freethought and Socialism" and he pointed to the widest aspects of the freethought tradition: "The driving force to save mankind must come from the freethinking tradition, from a tradition that preached internationalism at a time of internationalism. The next century of freethought must be the greatest of all, for the determination to speak freely alone can save us." (December, 1981.)

Jim Herrick, at that time editor, wrote in the centenary issue of the *Freethinker:*

> Two strands of secularism make it very important in the world of politics today: it is not revolutionary and utopian, and it is firmly committed to free inquiry. The Judaeo-Christian tradition is messianic — and secular versions of the messianic tradition have led to expectation of heaven or hell on earth. Secularists believe in neither. There is no expectation that revolution will suddenly produce a perfect world: that is why it is so important to reform and ameliorate the worst aspects of the world as we find it. Nor do secularists follow the inverted messianism of those who prophesy an imminent end to the world. Nuclear stock-piling and rampant pollution present problems on a scale not known hitherto. But they will not be solved by doom-and-gloom prophecies or romantic pastoral notions of starting society afresh. We must look at the human animal realistically, with both co-operative and selfish instincts, with potential for anger and tenderness, cruelty and kindness; and with realism, reason and imagination we must move forward from one problem to the next, from one reform to the next...
>
> The major issues of our time such as disarmament, race relations, unemployment and equable sharing of the world's resources of food and energy, do not allow us to look to the future with easy optimism. Freethought — "the best of causes" — will continue to clear the ground by exposing religions where they obscure issues and cloud thought. The secular humanist outlook — whatever phrase is used — will continue to provide an essential ingredient of civilisation. Long may the *Freethinker* flourish. (May, 1981.)

Chapman Cohen, in depressing circumstances during the Second World War, was challenged by a friendly critic to say what value the *Freethinker* had been to society. He replied, referring to the wide range of freethought journals that had come and gone:

> But of all these journals, past and present, is there one that has maintained continuously as high a standard as the *Freethinker* has done? This journal touches in turn almost every aspect of life, and it has done this without sinking into the mire of political advocacy, the useless pedantry of ethical learning, or the semi-religious unfruitfulness of mere teaching. The

> *Freethinker* has poured sarcasm on religion, but that has been the cover for knowledge, it has lifted fear from the minds of multitudes and kept its readers in close touch with the latest theories and knowledge of the origin, nature and the significance of the scientific study of religion. Quite as important has been the manner in which it has made plain the bearing of the survival of religious ideas on our social life and institutions. Let anyone pick up a volume of the *Freethinker* of any year, and he will see that I have not in the least overstated the facts. I think also it would be difficult to show that at any other time any other outspoken *Freethought* paper has been read in so many sections of society. And certainly if one takes a knowledge of the *Freethinker* to his reading of the papers up and down the country he will, if he knows it, think of Charles Lamb's description of books that are "damned good to steal from". (16 March, 1941.)

The final word must go to G.W. Foote, whose courage, breadth and literary power are all visible in his essay "The Gospel of Freethought". He opened:

> Christians are perpetually crying that we destroy and never build up. Nothing could be more false for all negation has a positive side, and we cannot deny error without affirming truth. But even if it were true, it would not lessen the value of our work. You must clear the ground before you can build, and plough before you can sow. Splendour gives no strength to an edifice whose foundations are treacherous, nor can a harvest be reaped from fields unprepared for the seeds.

He concluded:

> The only noble things in this world are great hearts and great brains. There is no virtue in a starveling piety which turns all beauty into ugliness and shrivels up every natural affection. Let the heart beat high with courage and enterprise, and throb with warm passion. Let the brain be an active engine of thought, imagination and will. The gospel of sorrow has had its day: the time has come for the gospel of gladness. Let us live out our lives to the full, radiating joy on all in our circle, and diffusing happiness through the grander circle of humanity, until at last we retire from the banquet of life, as others have done before us, and sink in eternal repose.

(First published in the *Freethinker*, 20 August, 1882; reprinted in *Flowers of Freethought*.)

BIBLIOGRAPHY

Susan Budd: Varieties of Unbelief, 1850 — 1960. Atheists and Agnostics in English Society, Heineman, 1977.

G.W. Foote: Flowers of Freethought. R. Forder, 1893.

A. Calder-Marshall: Lewd, Blasphemous and Obscene. Hutchinson, 1973.

George Meredith: Collected Letters, edited by his son. Constable, 1912.

Edward Royle: Victorian Infidels, 1891 — 1866. The Origins of the British Secularist Movement. Manchester University Press, 1971.
Radicals, Secularists and Republicans, Popular Freethought in Britain, 1866 — 1915. Manchester University Press, 1980.
Radical Politics, 1790 — 1900, Religion and Unbelief. (Documents with commentary) Longman, 1971.
The Infidel Tradition, From Paine to Bradlaugh. (Documents with commentary) Macmillan, 1976.

Nigel Sinnott: Joseph Symes, The "Flower of Atheism". Pamphlet published by the Atheist Society of Australia, 1977.

G.H. Taylor: A Chronology of British Secularism. National Secular Society, 1957.

David Tribe: President Charles Bradlaugh. Elek, 1971.
100 Years of Freethought. Elek, 1967.

J.M. Wheeler: Sixty Years of Freethought. The *Freethinker,* June, July 1897. Reprinted in An Anthology of Atheism and Rationalism. Edited by Gordon Stein. Prometheus Books, NY, USA, 1980.

INDEX